Gernot Candolini and Jennifer Brandon

PLACES *of* LIGHT

THE GIFT OF CATHEDRALS TO THE WORLD

mount
tabor
BOOKS

PARACLETE PRESS
BREWSTER, MASSACHUSETTS
BARGA, ITALY

2019 First Printing

Places of Light: The Gift of Cathedrals to the World

Copyright © 2019 by Gernot Candolini and Jennifer Brandon
Original German-language edition: Gernot Candolini, Die Kathedrale © 2017
Verlag Herder GmbH, Freiburg im Breisgau

ISBN 978-1-64060-176-5

Scripture translations and translations from other sources are the authors' own, even when a source citation may be furnished in the notes.

The Mount Tabor Books name and logo (mountain with rays of light) are trademarks of Paraclete Press, Inc.

Library of Congress Control Number: 2019944290

10 9 8 7 6 5 4 3 2 1

Published by Paraclete Press
Brewster, Massachusetts and Barga, Italy
www.paracletepress.com

Printed in Malaysia

CONTENTS

PREFACE

A cathedral can be defined in two ways. The scholarly definition is this: a church where a bishop teaches from the cathedra, a special chair in the altar area. The poetic definition is this: a large church that is a spiritual center for its community. Other cultures and languages have a separate word for this poetic definition. For example, in German the word "Dom" is used, and, similarly, "Duomo" in Italian. In this book, the word "cathedral" is meant in the wide, poetic sense with full understanding that some of the holy spaces featured do not carry the distinction of a "cathedral." Some of the mentioned buildings are basilicas, like Vézelay or Guadalupe, while others are simply large churches, like Ulm or Orleans, and the Hagia Sophia is now a museum.

Our intention for writing this book is that it may be like a "hyphen" between the readers and the cathedrals and churches. It wants to be a "heart warmer" and a song for the eyes and the soul that speak the words: There is something greater than we, and it is beautiful. There is a story and a history about the contact between us and God, and its message is this: we have a home.

We invite you to peek inside these awe-inspiring holy spaces in every way—into the beautiful physical structures, into the history that called them into being, and into the heart stories of the people who had the courage to see the process through. We hope that these pages fan the flame of curiosity that already dwells within you. It would be a bold statement indeed to suggest that we could offer answers about why these magnificent places have continued to be compelling to each generation over the last millennia. We believe that the answers are as diverse and dynamic as those who wander across a threshold and find themselves in a place that is wholly other. Instead, we have noticed that there are common threads and themes that connect these buildings, that inspire us to ask better questions, and cause us to wonder anew at the ever-unfolding relationship between God and the People of God.

But one thing we know for sure—after seeing saints and sinners, scientists and poets, theologians and people of the Bible in a variety of cathedrals painstakingly carved into stone and glass in order to preserve their stories and distill the truth of their lives—is that these vast and holy spaces have room for our stories too. Not only are they places of immense scale and grandeur, but also they act as a sort of living room, offering comfort for our earthly journey.

The beginnings of this project go back to a book first published in Germany; that earlier edition contained only the chapters of European cathedrals. Now, in the first English edition, the text of the chapters on the European cathedrals has been expanded, and chapters of places from the American continent have been added. We make no claim that the cathedrals chosen to grace the following pages somehow form a list of all the special churches in the world. On the contrary, we fully acknowledge it is not within our scope to document the many beautiful and beloved sacred spaces beyond this selection. Our hope is only that these few examples will encourage you to find more favorites and add them to your own inner book of powerful places that shelter or inspire your soul.

INTRODUCTION

Cathedrals are among the masterpieces of human architecture. Their size and grandeur are impressive and fascinating. They possess timeless charisma, even though, as with all things of this world, they have experienced declines and upswings as history has unfolded. Beyond their primary task of being the seat for religious liturgies and celebrations, cathedrals tend to attract people on the most ordinary of days. Many enter looking for a space for inner contemplation and prayer or simply to take in the astonishing views. Others seek out cathedrals as important tourist attractions that house masterpieces of art and precious relics, and then there are pilgrims who search for where the soul can be touched and inspired.

Many are drawn in by the majesty and abundance, the large gates, the colors, the profound silence, the faint echoes that wander through the vaults, and the resonance and solemnity of the vast spaces that give one the feeling of being surrounded by mystery. The compelling nature of these gentle giants continues as the seeker moves among the pillars; witnesses the harmonious beauty and clarity of light, the mastery of craftsmanship, and the great language of art and images; and ponders the abundance of perspectives and impressions. Even from the point of entry into the cathedral, visitors are surrounded by the powerful stories and presence of spiritual ancestors, which often give people a sense of their own being and place within the Greater Story, a sense that their soul is at home.

Cathedrals rise in the landscape of cities like pivot points or the hub of a wheel that gives a center around which everyday life revolves. At the same time, they are islands, places of silence, contemplation, and wonder. Even if a stream of visitors flows

Choir windows, Chartres Cathedral

through the church, silence and peace can be found there. The rooms inspire dialogue and provoke songs or prayers to rise into our consciousness.

Cathedrals stand at the crossroads of history, witnessing wealth and artistic power and the overwhelming desire to create something beautiful and magnificent. Buildings of this magnitude are always conceived and brought to fruition by many who gather around the vision and have the patience for the myriad steps involved. Some construction work lasts for centuries, while other buildings take only decades to complete. In Chartres during the twelfth century, the whole city rebuilt the cathedral by working together during a committed three-year period. Because of this unique initial energy, Chartres is the fastest-built Gothic cathedral in the world, with the roof having been completed just twenty-six years after the foundation stone was laid.

The order to build a cathedral is usually made by the bishop and the cathedral chapter, but there are always exceptions. In Barcelona, for example, even though a cathedral already existed in the city, the idea from a local bookseller to build another church, followed by donations, solidarity, and the mastery of the architect Antonio Gaudí, turned the proposed church dedicated to the Holy Family into one of the most remarkable sacred spaces in the world.

Cathedrals have also experienced the storms of history and survived them differently. Despite the iconoclasts of the Huguenot wars, the French Revolution, and the two world wars during which many cathedrals were damaged and some were even completely destroyed or demolished, most have survived the turmoil of conflicts and changing values surprisingly well.

Throughout history, cathedrals have continued to stir something inside passersby and the faithful alike: a common feeling of admiration, wonder, joy, reverence, and the desire that these special places continue to stand as witnesses and storytellers to future generations.

"And this has been standing here for centuries. The premier work of man perhaps in the whole Western world, and it's without a signature: Chartres. A celebration to God's glory and to the dignity of man. All that's left, most artists seem to feel these days, is man. Naked, poor, forked radish. There aren't any celebrations. Ours, the scientists keep telling us, is a universe which is disposable. You know, it might be just this one anonymous glory of all things, this rich stone forest, this epic chant, this gaiety, this grand, choiring shout of affirmation, which we choose when all our cities are dust, to stand intact, to mark where we have been, to testify to what we had it in us to accomplish."

—Orson Welles,
American film actor and director

1

COLOGNE CATHEDRAL

C ologne Cathedral is one with a long history of building. More than six hundred years passed between the laying of the foundation stone in the thirteenth century and the completion of the building in the nineteenth century. During half of this long spell the construction was at a halt, but then renewed interest and energy came in the 1800s for finishing what had been started so long before. Now it stands as one of the most recognized landmarks in Germany. Among the important relics housed here are links from the chain of St. Peter and a piece of the True Cross, as well as a miraculous image of Mary called the Schmuck (Jewelled) Madonna. But the most significant treasure of all to come to Cologne arrived from the Holy Land in the twelfth century following a crusade: the relics of the Three Wise Men, the Magi from the East who traveled to visit and bring gifts to the Christ Child. The reliquary that contains their precious remains is one of the most superb works of gold in the world, and the reason that the current cathedral was built was to provide an appropriately glorious shelter for such cherished relics.

Dedicated to St. Peter and the Virgin Mary, the cathedral itself looks like a manifestation of strength and greatness, almost menacing with its darkened stone and enormous dimension. The soaring vaults combine with the intricate filigree details to symbolize both the determination and joy of creating something magnificent. However, the story of the cathedral construction is laborious and long. Initially, only the choir and part of the south tower were built. The medieval crane erected at the top of the tower stood there for

◀ *Cologne Cathedral and the bridge over the Rhine river*

five hundred years and for a long time was part of the skyline of Cologne. The people of Cologne used to say, "Before the cathedral is finished, the world goes under." When Napoleon occupied the city in 1794, he used the cathedral as a horse stable and warehouse. But in the nineteenth century, a new enthusiasm for the Gothic style developed, and the people of Cologne decided to finish the work. The carefully preserved original plans from the thirteenth century were again used to guide the process. Finally, the nave, which had only been partially constructed up to that point, could be finished and the "temporary" wall that had been set up in front of the choir was removed. After more than six centuries, the long-awaited cathedral could be experienced in its entirety. In 1880, with the completion of both towers, there was an official opening ceremony, and for a short time Cologne Cathedral enjoyed being the tallest building in the world, eclipsed by the Washington Monument and the Eiffel Tower in 1884.

It was a difficult time during World War II, as the old city of Cologne and the cathedral were bombed numerous times. Although it is situated right beside the railway station and a strategically important bridge over the Rhine river, it is likely that the cathedral was not completely destroyed precisely because it was such an easily distinguishable landmark for pilots from the air. Still, a separate group of guards, known as the Domwächter, were necessary for the purpose of extinguishing as soon as possible the incendiary bombs that hit the cathedral. After the war, a rapid renovation to restore the damage from the bombings was successful. However, it was noticed that the softer stone used in parts of the earlier efforts to complete the building was succumbing to weather erosion, and the renovation to

Detail, Golden Shrine of the Three Kings, Cologne Cathedral ▶

COLOGNE CATHEDRAL

repair these areas continues today. The people of Cologne have always managed to keep their treasure secure in times of uncertainty and danger.

It seems this work will never be completely finished. However, the visitors of today do not notice much of it. The magnificent building is waiting to be visited; light shines through its partly modern windows. Particularly noteworthy are the "Richter windows," which were executed like a modern pixel image. This seems unusual at first glance, but if one observes the play of colors on the columns, one notices how modern forms can create touching beauty. Today, Cologne Cathedral is not only a World Heritage Site and the most visited church in Germany but also an elaborate space for celebration of spirit and faith.

"Human nature took its highest effort when it thought of a Gothic cathedral in perfection, but they remained an ideal, and rightly so, for the perfected must remain unfinished: the finished Gothic cathedrals are not perfect, and the perfect ones are not finished."

—Theodor Fontane,
nineteenth-century German poet

COLOGNE CATHEDRAL

◀ *Vault, Cologne Cathedral*

Construction Plan of a Rose Window

2

THE CATHEDRAL BUILDERS

The construction of a cathedral is a logistical master-piece. The artistic and technical organization of material requirements and the details of catering to the workers' needs contribute to an often-humming hive of activity. As part of a large construction site, it was common that in the shadow of a rising cathedral corresponding structures were also erected that housed the different trades necessary for building. Craftspeople were organized into guilds, among which the stonemasons held a special position. They were the key to mastering the technical and artistic challenges, and they had to have expertise that required special training and responsibility. The masons designed their own rules and formed brotherhoods through which a deep bond between master and student was fostered. Expertise was carefully passed on only to those in the community, giving it the aura of secret knowledge. Measures and numbers, and laws of harmony and statics, were elements of the specialized knowledge learned by those who were prepared to engage in long training within a binding community.

The brotherhoods referred to the archetypes of sacred architec-ture, such as Solomon's Temple. They studied the given measurements in the Old Testament and gleaned out of it a divine order, as well as the harmonic laws of music from Pythagoras. For them, music and architecture were closely connected; each room serves as a sound space, specifically aligned with the laws of harmony in order to accommodate both spoken word and music. The masters also studied the revelation of John and his vision of the New Jerusalem. Everything that is said there in terms of architectural statements was questioned as to whether it could be implemented in the present, as a kind of foresight of the heavenly Jerusalem, in part or in full. The three gates of the heavenly Jerusalem became the three portals that form the entrances to the cathedrals, and the walls described, sparkling like gems, were imitated in the glass windows.

The brotherhood of the stonemasons usually provided the architect and organized the other artisans. Carpenters, glassmakers, painters, and the various guilds were subordinate to him. In the Romanesque and early Gothic, the names of master masons, architects, or artists had no meaning. The individual stepped back in humility behind the complete work. It was self-evident that a person's artistry is a gift from God and not the merit of an individual. On only a few occasions from that period did individual names of architects or master masons appear.

It is remarkable that so many cathedrals could be built in small towns. In France alone there were over fifty. Due to the central importance of the church in the early European Middle Ages, all resources were taken into account during the construction of an impressive church. Everyone joined together, all donations flowed into a single project, all craftsmanship focused on one place. Thus, they left us a legacy that still today can fill us with wonder and appreciation.

When people left Europe to seek a better fortune in the new countries of North and South America, they wanted to build places of gathering and worship in their new homes. They started with churches for small congregations, but then the wish for having a big cathedral became strong in the big cities. Again, money was collected, mostly private sponsors who gave all that was needed to build the grand space. The Gothic style was again popular because of its wonderful lines, the symphonies of colored light in the windows, and the upwardly rising structures. The American cathedrals are young when compared to those of their European predecessors, but they might stand as the others have for hundreds and maybe thousands of years, uplifting the generations that have built them and used them, and uplifting those generations yet to come.

Abbey Church, Pontigny, France ▷

"Perfect proportions led builders of great churches to conceive of architecture as applied geometry, geometry as applied theology, and the designer of a Gothic cathedral as an imitator of the divine Master."

—Robert A. Scott,
professor and president of Adelphi University in New York

3

ST. STEPHEN'S CATHEDRAL

Saint Stephen's Cathedral in Vienna is commonly known to the Viennese as Steffl ("Steve"), a name that accurately conveys the emotional and friendly connection they feel toward their main church. The Gothic nave was first built in the fifteenth century around an old Romanesque church that was partially demolished during construction. In contrast to many other cathedrals, St. Stephen's Cathedral has preserved an extensive amount of its original architectural plans. When completed in 1433, the South Tower was for some time the tallest church tower in the world. The square layout of the tower is gradually transformed into an octagon by the ingenious arrangement of gables and turrets. Its top is crowned by a cross worn by the Habsburg double-headed eagle. Special features of the cathedral are the colorful patterns and coat of arms of the colored glazed roof shingles. Also famous is the Gothic pulpit, which is considered a masterpiece of stonemasonry. In the foot of the pulpit, a man looks out of a window. Here, the stonemason has brought to life a figure with an expression known as the "window gawk," with which the Viennese of certain eras were likely to identify. It was a common habit, for example, in times before television entered modern life, to lean at the windowsill and watch the goings on in the street below.

Another special feature is the choir, turned about one degree off the axis. The turn causes the light to shine straight into the church on St. Stephen's Day, December 26th, illuminating the icon of Stephen. The bell of the cathedral, the so-called Pummerin, or "Boomer," is well known across Austria. It is the third largest free-swinging bell in the world after the bell cast in 2016 for the Orthodox cathedral in Bucharest—the People's Salvation Cathedral, which is still under construction—and the "Dicker Pitter" in Cologne. It rings only on special feast days, including every year at midnight on New Year's Eve, when it is broadcast on national radio. The deep peal of the Pummerin is recognized by listeners throughout Austria.

In the destruction of the Second World War, the cathedral roof burned down and several vaults collapsed. Throughout Austria, money was collected for the comprehensive restoration work of the cathedral. Each federal state contributed to the effort, demonstrating how many Austrians perceived St. Stephen's Cathedral as the architectural and spiritual heart of their country.

It is a special feeling to sit on one of the benches of this cathedral and imagine that Wolfgang Amadeus Mozart was married there, and that he conducted concerts in that space. Josef and Michael Haydn, too, and Franz Schubert sang in the boys' choir; Anton Bruckner played the famous organ. Also, the funeral of Antonio Vivaldi took place in St. Stephen's, and legend says that Ludwig van Beethoven's total deafness first became apparent to him when he observed birds flying away from the tower yet could not hear the sound of the bells ringing.

St. Stephen's Cathedral, perhaps more than other cathedrals because of Vienna's singular ability to become home for world-class musicians, is woven into the very fabric of music history. Still, it remains a home for all who enter. People of all backgrounds—artists and craftspeople, royals and beggars, dignitaries and asylum seekers, children and the elderly, locals and tourists—find resonance within its walls.

"The cathedral is not a static, self-contained building; in it is movement, dynamics. It appeals to people to understand themselves as travelers traveling to a destination, to God dwelling in the light. Man, in the shadow of the death of the West, is called to make the journey into the kingdom of God. The cathedral shows him the way to the sunrise, to the East, to the Holy of Holies, to the eternal light."

—Christoph Schönborn,
Archbishop of Austria

ST. STEPHEN'S
CATHEDRAL

4

WASHINGTON NATIONAL CATHEDRAL

When the United States of America was founded, it was clear it should have a capital. A site was chosen on the Potomac River, between Maryland and Virginia, and then began the construction of a completely new town on this expanse of marshland. Even in this early beginning, the idea of building a cathedral was discussed. For this purpose, a century later, a hill was chosen, Mount St. Alban, which is the highest point overlooking the nation's capital.

Originally the cathedral was envisioned as a large, domed building. However, shortly before construction began in 1907 it was decided the cathedral should not be built in a Renaissance style after all, but rather as a Gothic cathedral. The opinion was that Gothic, like no other form of architecture, is capable of elevating, pleasing, and bringing visitors into a world of wonder and adoration. It was finally completed in 1990, making it "the cathedral of the twentieth century," encapsulating both the thoughts and style of the time. As in the medieval era, the building was born of great visions by a multitude of highly esteemed and devoted people. And, despite the impression one receives from its name, this cathedral was constructed entirely from private gifts and donations.

Although many architects were involved, it was Philip Hubert Frohman who captured its vision. Frohman felt his first passion for building a Gothic cathedral at the age of seven. He entered college at the age of eleven, and by sixteen, he had received his architecture degree. By age thirty-four, he had come full circle to his childhood

dream and signed the contract to be Washington National Cathedral's chief architect, a position he would hold for the next half century.

Washington National Cathedral is unlike any other church; it stands as a wonderful recent example of Gothic architecture. It is the synthesis of talented people who knew how to work with light, color, form, and beauty. With great pride, the people of Washington often praise their cathedral with remarks such as this one, attributed to Robert Mark, an emeritus professor of civil engineering and architecture at Princeton University: "As long as earthquakes or mankind don't knock it down, it will stand, without further reinforcement, for the better part of the next two millennia."

Unexpectedly, and without precedent in the modern era, a severe earthquake occurred in the Washington area in August 2011. Few had considered that this part of the earth would be in danger of major ground shifts. Nonetheless, the magnitude 5.8 tremor caused the cathedral's buttresses to crack, large limestone pinnacles to twist, and some of the hand-carved finials to fall from the towers. Repair work is still underway, but the cathedral that might stand forever has suffered the innermost crack of finiteness.

Even still, the dancing light keeps descending into this place on every sunny day like a fountain of joy, with the colors caressing and cascading down the walls. The wise visitor will eventually put the camera away, realizing that it is futile to accurately capture in the lens the wonder of this holy space. The better choice is to enjoy this wonderful gift with your own eyes and notice how the light makes its way into your soul.

Those who slowly take in the beautiful art may at first be attracted by the sweet and also spectacular stories of the windows. To pay tribute to the time when this church was built, the Apollo missions to the moon found their way into the memories of time that fill the windows. This striking window features a red-colored orb, in the center of which there is a small white circle surrounding a black basalt moon rock. The stone was brought back to earth by the first crew that landed on the moon and was directly attached into the window.

◁ *Nave, Washington National Cathedral*

The west rose is a swirling pool of creation, water and fire, glitter and sparkle. It is the masterpiece of Rowan LeCompte, who, either alone or partnering with his wife, Irene, designed a total of forty-two windows in the church. Some of his best are seen in the series of nave clerestory windows with their bright and vivid colors. One after another they invite the viewer to want to know more about the stories they tell, and they inspire some to feel a greater interest and deeper attachment to this astonishing structure. Time is required to take it all in. More than one visit is necessary because this cathedral never ceases to reveal something beautiful and new.

As serious as this national monument is, like most every great work of art, it contains delightful details that, when noticed, bring a twinkle to the eye and a smile in the heart. Thus, visitors may now spy in the far reaches of the stone walls a unicorn, a glutton, a hippie, a yuppie, and of course as tribute to this city, a politician. Later, as the result of a schoolchildren's contest, the lost son of the universe was added and Darth Vader was placed on the northwest tower. May the Force be with him and us! A visionary place will always make space to include children, and therefore Children's Chapel with a lower ceiling and appropriately tiny chairs is among a row of many different and welcoming chapels. Others include a place to pay tribute to veterans, as well as saints such as Mary and John.

Washington National Cathedral is a national house of prayer and service. It welcomes everyone and offers a shelter of structure and strength, light and enlightenment, freedom and peace. People are invited in moments of celebration, joy, sorrow, and solemnity to be connected with the Greater Story and the joy of being a pilgrim on this earth within the wondrous history of the universe and humankind.

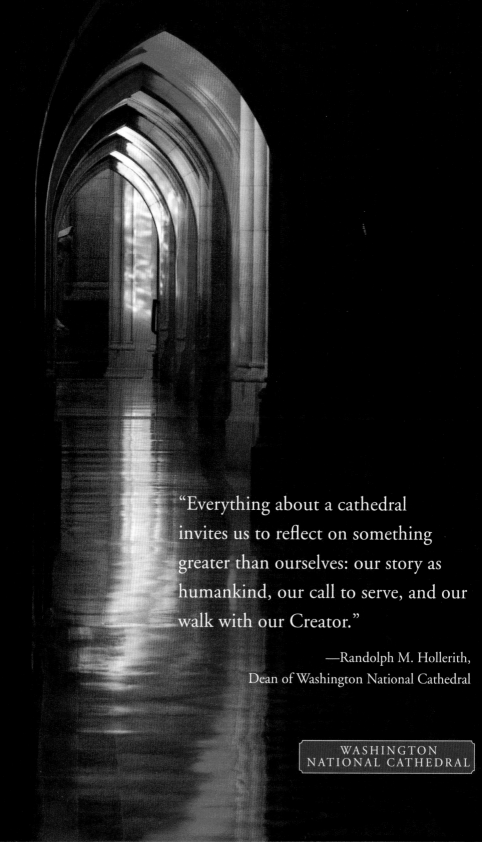

"Everything about a cathedral invites us to reflect on something greater than ourselves: our story as humankind, our call to serve, and our walk with our Creator."

—Randolph M. Hollerith,
Dean of Washington National Cathedral

WASHINGTON
NATIONAL CATHEDRAL

5

REIMS CATHEDRAL

Reims breathes French history like no other place. It was here in 499 that the first Frankish King, Clovis, was baptized and anointed with holy oil. Subsequently, most of the French kings were crowned here.

In 1211, construction began on a Gothic cathedral that was to be worthy of the festive services and honorable ceremonies that already had centuries of history in this community. While the nave was completed after 100 years, the towers and other exterior components were never fully completed. The Gothic technique of distributing the load of the roof onto many pillars frees the walls from their supporting function, so they can be filled with impressive glass windows and delicate tracery. Even today, the joy of the builders can be imagined as always ready to create new and more beautiful and coherent dresses and patterns, while simultaneously possessing the ability to insert every detail into a large, fully organic building.

During World War I, the building was almost completely destroyed. Because Reims Cathedral was synonymous with the long history of strength of the French, it became the target of German attackers. Many glass windows were destroyed, the attic was burned down, and portions of the cathedral collapsed. After the war, the damage could only be slowly and painstakingly removed. The destroyed roof was renewed with concrete struts, and many broken figures were copied and newly chiseled.

On June 8, 1962, a significant new beginning came when the German chancellor and the French president met for Mass

◀ *Windows by Imi Knoebel, Reims Cathedral*

Window by Marc Chagall, Reims Cathedral

within these storied walls. This meeting was the symbolic prelude to the reconciliation process between Germany and France. On the floor of the cathedral, a tablet was inscribed with the words:

Your Excellency, the Chancellor
Konrad Adenauer and I are coming
into your Cathedral to seal the
reconciliation between
France and Germany.
~Charles de Gaulle

In 1974, the renowned twentieth-century Jewish artist Marc Chagall was invited to design the windows in the front chapel. His art, in its own ethereal manner, is now one of the attractions of the cathedral. To the left and right of the middle chapel, the German artist Imi Knoebel has designed the other chapel windows as counterpoints using shattered glass of striking, strong colors.

The symbolism of this arrangement is a vivid sign of reconciliation: a Jewish artist in the center chapel, accompanied by a German artist, all within this magnificent French cathedral. It creates a strong statement for today and for future generations that even after a long history of war, pain, and destruction, peace and friendship are possible.

Window by Imi Knoebel ▲
and reconciliation tablet,
Reims Cathedral

À MONSEIGNEUR MARTY
ARCHEVÊQUE DE REIM

'EXCELLENCE, LE CHANCELIE
ADENAUER ET MOI-MÊM
VENONS DANS VOT
CATHÉDRALE SCELL
LA RÉCONCILIATION DE
FRANCE ET DE L'ALLEMA

CHARLES DE GAU
DIMANCHE 8 JUILLET 1962

Despite its varied history and its long construction period that has never come to completion, Reims remains one of the greatest works of the Gothic arts. The towering west facade with its two rose windows is one of the most impressive entrances in the world; passing through it is truly a "royal" experience for every human being. The towers, with their graceful tracery, are manifestations of steadfastness and strength. The more than 2,000 carved figures are not only a symphony of stonemasonry, but also a great setting of all the spiritual fathers and mothers gathered for each service, feast, visit, and celebration in their symbolic presence.

Among all these figures, there is one that particularly catches the eye. It is most frequently represented on postcards, coins, books, and is considered the messenger of Reims. Its face is one of the most inviting and sympathetic in art history. The smiling angel on the left portal has triggered a smile back from innumerable visitors, and has aroused phrases such as, "If God's angels look at me like this and welcome me so generously when my earthly life is ended, then all will indeed be well."

"It is a royal cathedral,
a martyred cathedral:
an epic tale."

—From a home page of Reims Cathedral

◀ *Gutter with wolf and musician*
The double rose of Reims Cathedral ▶

REIMS CATHEDRAL

6

THE SMILING STONES

The great portals of cathedrals are filled with the standing witnesses of kings and queens, elders and saints, apostles and prophets. These significant pillars of our faith remind us of the story from which we came and accompany us in our thoughts and reflections. Their myriad experiences and life lessons make them patrons and patronesses for our own paths toward transformation. From them we can learn and be inspired for that journey.

One striking aspect of the figures is their diversity. Of course, Jesus and the apostles are represented, but among them also are Abraham with Sarah and Hagar, David and Bathsheba, and Solomon and the Queen of Sheba. Together with major prophets such as Isaiah and Jeremiah, one may spy a Roman sibyl, one of the prophetesses that one can see even on the ceiling of the Sistine Chapel. Hannah and Simeon's gazes still recognize the Messiah in the infant Jesus, as does Elizabeth, the mother of John the Baptist and an important companion of Mary. There is Mary herself, along with Anne, Mary's mother, and still others: the mysterious priest Melchizedek, Elijah, Aaron and Moses, bishops and martyrs.

In Chartres Cathedral, even Pythagoras and Aristotle have gathered, certainly a unique feature of the cosmopolitan Chartres school. But also in other places some unusual patrons stand steadfastly, including Virgil and Cicero in the choir stalls of Ulm.

The patrons are saints not because they lived a perfect life, but because of their deep humanity. They are not supermen and

The smiling angel at the gate of Reims Cathedral

women without stains, but grandfathers and grandmothers who have indeed carved out something great in their lives, flaws and failures notwithstanding. They represent every kind of human experience—vision and prophecy, fear and doubt, anger and violence, reconciliation and peace, desire and sacrifice, compassion and tenderness. Common to all is the willingness to listen, and confidence in the presence of God and in God's faithful interaction in the human adventure. And because there are so many different patrons, each pilgrim can be drawn to the one who helps her or him to cross over a threshold and open another door.

These figures were made by various artists. Some—depending on age, style, and craftsmanship—are graceful or clumsy, static or lively. Then there are those that were obviously created by great master stonemasons, who could conjure up different forms of expression in the attitude and facial features in such a delicate and subtle way that it is as if the figures were still alive. Often it is the little but beguiling hint of a smile playing on the stone faces that compels the onlooker to smile right back.

Somehow, we are wondrously drawn to the faces of the Angel of Reims, James of Paris, Solomon and the Queen of Sheba in Chartres. How can stone be so alive? How can characters be so beautiful that you wish they would descend and have a conversation? But they stand still, lofty and upright, quietly burning inside like candles that light the way into the house of God. And when we return to the world, they seem to look after us and send their blessings upon us to accomplish what lies before us in our everyday lives.

Donatus, patron of Grammar at Chartres Cathedral ▶

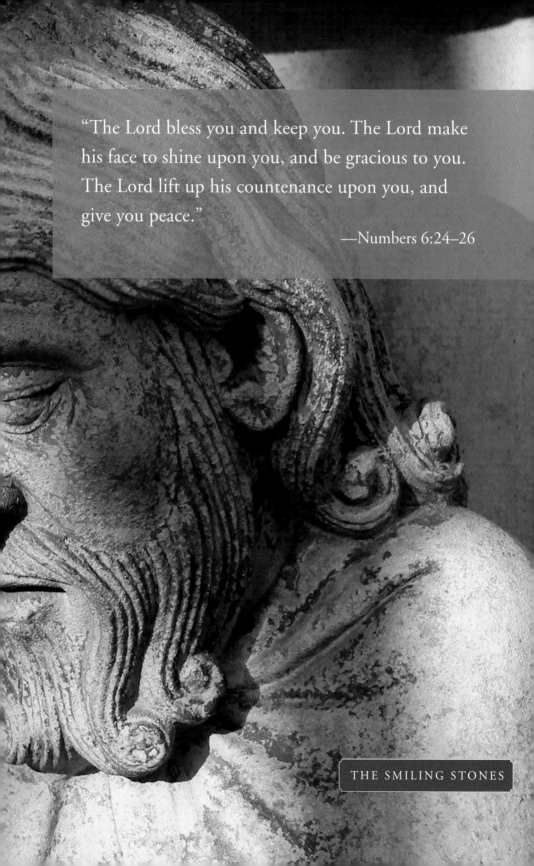

"The Lord bless you and keep you. The Lord make his face to shine upon you, and be gracious to you. The Lord lift up his countenance upon you, and give you peace."

—Numbers 6:24–26

THE SMILING STONES

7

CLUNY ABBEY AND TAIZÉ

The monastic order of the Benedictines has decisively shaped monasticism particular to Christianity in its simple principles. If one directs one's life fully to God and places it completely in the service of faith, then one renounces possessions, marriage and children, and the freedom to choose for oneself. Poverty, celibacy, and obedience are the basis of all monastic commitment. Benedict of Nursia, founder of the Benedictines, set other special emphases in his monastic Rule, as well, that still have relevance today. More than a third of the Rule deals with the abbot and rules for good leadership. Humility is given particular attention.

There are also passages known far beyond the Benedictines. "Pray and work" is perhaps the shortest expression of the universal principle of the balance of action and contemplation, doing and letting go, engaging in activity and resting, acting and being. Also, the opening word of the Benedictine Rule: "Incline the ear of your heart" is an expression of universal humanity and listening to the inner voice of intuition. It suggests turning to one another with affection as the basic form of love.

In the course of history, some monasteries crept into an arbitrariness and negligence that challenged individual monks, as well as whole groups, to reinterpret the Rule in its consistency and clarity. Two major reforms renewed the Benedictines during the Middle Ages: the reform of Cluny and the reform of the Cistercians. As a result of the first, the monastery of Cluny became a remarkable place. In its prime, Cluny had more than

The last standing tower of Cluny Abbey

1,000 monks. Not only did they build the largest cathedral in the world, they also built Europe's first major social movement. Up to 25,000 poor people were cared for at the same time by the Cluny religious, who nursed the sick and set up a network of social services.

But every blossom fades. Throughout history, the Church has often become alienated from the needs of the people. For instance, in French absolutism, the clergy were in lockstep solidarity with the rulers and not with the poor. That is why in France not only the king and his lofty nobility were swept away in the French Revolution, but also the Church. The people's anger at the ruling class was so profound that the destruction of buildings and churches reached unimaginable proportions.

In the wake of the French Revolution in 1793, the Abbey of Cluny was abolished and its property confiscated. The monastery church was initially still intact. But under the rule of Napoleon, in 1810, large parts were blown up to be used as a quarry for the construction of a horse breeding station and other buildings. The loss of this largest and perhaps most beautiful Romanesque church in the world hurts to this day. Only a single small tower of the aisle survived the demolition. (Recently, a 3D animation was created by which one can at least guess what a great cathedral Cluny once was.)

But where the spirit blows, something stays and seeks new ways. The flower fades or is crushed, but seed still secretly falls back into the earth to break out anew. From ruins, new life grows. In the last century, right next to Cluny a new spring sprouted.

A group of young men gathered at this special place during the Second World War to found the Taizé Community. At first the brothers took care of war refugees, but then they began to invite young people. Inviting, listening, and being able to cope with life without great demands, this peaceful community of the first ecumenical fraternity in church history still influences the spirituality of thousands of people throughout Europe.

Chapel of Taizé

The most powerful charisma of Taizé are the songs and the singing—as if the old Latin chorales of the monks were heard out of the wind, rewritten by a musician of our days. How could Jacques Berthier and others compose such a multitude of little musical masterpieces if they were not sensitive and listening to a place that was and is home to the soul like few places in this world? "Laudate omnes gentes," "Ubi caritas," "In the Lord," "Confitemini Domino," "Within our darkest night," and many other songs have flown out like dandelion seeds from Taizé to find a place in the songs of other churches and communities throughout the world.

It is as if the ancient opening phrase of the Benedictines, "Incline the ear of your heart," still vibrates like a secret sound between the last remaining ruins of the great Abbey Church of Cluny to resonate in all who chant the songs of Taizé.

"Within our darkest night,
Lord, you kindle a fire that never dies away,
that never dies away."

—Jacques Berthier, composer of Taizé songs

Vézelay Basilica on the Hill of Joy

8

VÉZELAY BASILICA

Visible from all directions, the basilica known as La Madeleine of Vézelay is located on a hill that the pilgrims called "Mountain of Joy." Today, visitors from the parking lot at the foot of the hill go up the alley through the small town until, at last, they reach the crown jewel at the summit. After visitors enter the large narthex, their first glimpse catches the soaring heights of one of the most beautiful displays of Romanesque architecture still existing. The simple design—the most striking feature of which is the arches built with a sequence of white and red stones—makes the room look like a large, tightly stretched cloth.

Again in Vézelay, light is of central importance. Depending on the sun and the weather, light plays in the room, making it seem mysteriously dim or radiant. At certain times, the light compositions are led to impressive climaxes, such as on June 21, when points of light, which were dancing throughout the year on the walls and floors, are suddenly united in a row down the center aisle. A path then clearly leads a pilgrim to the heart of the church.

At the winter solstice, the light falls on the upper capitals of the columns. Within this limited portion of the columns is found the only adornments in the basilica, where scenes from the biblical stories, representations of the seasons, and allegories dance across the stones.

Just beyond the altar, the Gothic choir, added later, reaches even further toward heaven, where ethereal light pours through the towering clear glass and reflects off every surface. Seldom do two different architectural styles fit together as well as here, for both serve equally the light and the mystery of enlightenment.

In stark contrast to the soaring, light-filled church is the crypt that lies just below ground level. With its low ceiling and rough, uncut floor, it gives the impression of a natural cave where each step must be carefully taken. Within the crypt there are unusually slender pillars, as well, which are the supports for the chancel area of the church above. They seem rather unbalanced for holding up so many tons of stone, but they have nonetheless stood for better or worse for centuries on end. And yet, for all its peculiarities, a special niche in the back of the crypt contains the reason for this glorious space in the first place: relics of Mary Magdalene.

The biblical narratives speak of several Marys, and it is unclear if they represent different women or if the stories overlap into the same person. What *is* clear is that the one known as Mary of Magdala was healed by Jesus of demons. Apparently, she developed a special bond with Jesus as she began to follow him in his ministry, because in the end we find her standing at the foot of the cross with Jesus's other beloved ones, namely Mary, his mother, and John. And ultimately, all four Gospel writers named Mary Magdalene as the first person to witness the Resurrection. As she stood face to face with the risen Christ, he specifically told her to hurry and tell the other disciples this good news.

Because of this important distinction she holds, some later generations have named her the apostle to the apostles. Mary Magdalene was the first to break the story that would forever change the human landscape on earth. In many ways, the Basilica of Vézelay is a physical representation of her life. From the rough-hewn disarray and darkness of the crypt to the gloriously dancing light that leads the way to the Eucharist table, this holy space beautifully brings together the tension that is so evident and endearing to this singular woman. We can easily see ourselves in her, regardless of the point on the dark/light spectrum at which we are momentarily residing.

Perhaps it is because of this compelling and hopeful energy that seems to permeate every inch of the basilica that such a radiant space has witnessed legendary history. Both the Second and Third Crusades were launched from this hill, first with Bernard of Clairvaux preaching on the ramparts of Vézelay in the shadow of the basilica still in the process of being built. Then in 1190 King Richard the Lionheart of England and King Philip Augustus of France gathered their knights there to begin the journey toward Jerusalem.

More recently, in 1946, the year of the 800th anniversary of Bernard's electrifying words that ignited a Crusade, songs of peace were sung instead in the aftermath of World War II by tens of thousands of pilgrims. This was an overwhelming response to an earlier call by forty French bishops for a joint "Crusade of reconciliation between Germany and France." People from all over Europe arrived in Vézelay carrying wooden crosses in definitive support of this cause, and some of them can still be found in the aisles of the basilica.

The Basilica of Vézelay remains the goal of many pilgrims. A moving example of this can be seen every All Saints' Day, when some 2,500 Raiders (grown-up Boy Scouts) walk from all directions and ascend the hill of Vézelay. Knocking on the great front doors, they enter in a swell through the opening, all the while singing with strength and fervor. They also come seeking reconciliation and offering prayers for peace.

In the fragility of life, we can easily vacillate between that which terrorizes us and that which offers beauty. In the presence of such a profound place, we are reminded that the sun always rises to shine, and that tangled shadows will eventually become a trail of light leading us home. Today in Vézelay, the Community of Jerusalem prays the liturgy of the hours, and in the morning, they sing these verses from the Gospel of Luke:

"By the tender mercy of our God, the dawn from on high will break upon us, to give light to those who sit in darkness and in the shadow of death, to guide our feet into the way of peace."

—Luke 1:78–79

▲ *The famous "Mystic Mill" capital in Vézelay Basilica*
The plan for Vézelay Basilica nave

The path of light in Vézelay Basilica ▶

VÉZELAY BASILICA

9

THE WAY DOWN

Most cathedrals have a crypt, or a subspace, that leads visitors into the depths. These lower churches are much darker, sometimes cavernous spaces where the hustle and bustle of daily life quickly falls away. They are an underworld that holds open sacred space for contemplation. Sometimes silence settles in upon the visitor like a damp, heavy blanket, offering an invitation to slow down and encounter the darker and deeper sides of life.

In the crypt of Chartres Cathedral is an ancient deep well that predates Christianity, extending twenty-eight meters (92 feet) down to the water level. Originally healing water spilled there, and in the elongated crypt, countless pilgrims of the Middle Ages would spend a novena—a period of nine days in prayer, petition, and worship—in this womblike cave, with the hope of being healed. A black Madonna was placed at a high point, seeming to be somehow watching through her closed eyes over all who entered, as though she were perceiving and absorbing everything and sharing in the burdens of all who sought her help.

Many crypts serve as a burial ground, often where bishops or other important people are buried.

The crypt of St. Peter's Basilica entombs the bishops of Rome, who of course are the men who have held the office of pope. Another notable crypt is located near Paris in the Cathedral of Saint-Denis, where many French royalty are buried, including King Louis XVI and Marie Antoinette. The story of King Philip I seems almost ironic. He was buried by his own will in 1108 not in

Saint-Denis, but in the monastery of Saint-Benoît-sur-Loire. His grave is the only royal shrine of a king of France still preserved in its original state, because while all the tombs in Saint-Denis were looted during the French Revolution, the monastery was not touched.

As mentioned in the previous chapter, the crypt in Vézelay is unusual and somehow seems to fit perfectly with what is known about Mary Magdalene. With its uneven floor and spindly pillars, it exudes a sense of strength whose source is not readily apparent. There are a few places within the space where "daylight" windows allow light to stream in from the church above, making this submerged area brighter than most crypts. Mary Magdalene's strong, tender, and mysterious history hinted at in the four Gospels makes her a beloved saint whose patronage extends especially to those seeking wisdom in all manners of loving.

Life happens both in the light and in the dark. The word "crypt" means *hidden*, and many lower churches offer a safe place for dealing with those things in life that require only the faintest of light.

Sometimes dark, deep quiet is just the environment needed to see clearly.

"Deep in our soul is the desire to be accompanied, and to feel secure in the dark and uncertain. We wish to be strengthened and blessed by our ancestors and those who lived before us. Our hope is that this security is always and unconditionally there."

—Helge Burggrabe,
German composer and musician

THE WAY DOWN

10

DESTRUCTION
AND RECONCILIATION

When a great piece of art or architecture that represents thousands of hours of work, craftsmanship, faith, love, and reverence is destroyed, it shatters not only physical matter but also sends shock waves through the depths of many souls.

Grief casts long shadows over whole nations when precious art, or a great church, or a statue is blown up, destroyed, or badly damaged.

In September 1914, when the German army bombarded Reims Cathedral with shells and the glass windows shattered, stone figures fell, the attic began to burn as the molten lead flowed out of the dragon gargoyles on the eaves of the roof, and the North Tower threatened to collapse, it was an assault directly felt in the hearts of the people. In a similar way, then, the hollowed-out shell of the remaining church continued to accurately portray the emotional state of the community.

Few pictures of the Second World War have been as deeply impressed into the consciousness of the German people as the black and lonely towering Cologne Cathedral in the middle of a desert of rubble and ashes. Like a watchman whose shift is never complete, it seemed to survey the entire land, symbolizing, in the midst of the continent's greatest catastrophe, how terrible and bitter the destruction was.

The ruins of Cologne in 1945

When the roof of St. Stephen's Cathedral began to burn and collapsed during the last days of the war in April 1945 during the battle for Vienna, the bell tower also caught fire. The huge bell there, the *Pummerin*, plunged into the depths and shattered. The "Voice of Austria," which rang only on a few special holidays a year, had fallen silent.

In November 1940, Coventry Cathedral was completely destroyed by a German air raid. Only a single back wall of the sanctuary remained standing. Only a month later during his Christmas sermon, the Provost of the Cathedral, Richard Howard, said: "When all this is over, we must reach out to our enemies and build a more friendly world with them, in the spirit of Christ the Child." He is responsible for the words "Father, forgive" to be engraved in the last standing remains of the wall.

After the war, one of the most important reconciliation movements in Europe developed from Coventry. From three nails found in the rubble a cross was built. It has been copied many times and given to other churches throughout Europe, including the Wilhelm Memorial Church in Berlin. The result was the Nail-Cross Movement that

The roof of St. Stephen's Cathedral in Vienna after the fire

brought people together in prayers for peace, and continues to actively promote peace and reconciliation today. Coventry also spearheaded town twinning arrangements with a total of fifty-seven cities, including Dresden, as a concrete sign of the struggle for connection and reconciliation instead of separation and destruction.

In 1957, the newly cast Viennese *Pummerin* was raised at the north tower of the renovated St. Stephen's Cathedral. Its sound has now embedded itself in the Austrian soul like no other bell sound. Every year on New Year's Eve the ringing of the *Pummerin* is transmitted through the radio stations of Austria. A countdown of 5-4-3-2-1 is followed by a brief silence and then the ringing of the bell, the warm, deep sounds slowly flowing over into the Danube waltz, mixed with the feelings of the past year, as the joy, sadness, and gratitude and hope for a happy new year resonate in the souls of many Austrians.

In 1946, the newly formed Catholic peace organization Pax Christi called for a *Croisade de la Paix*—a Crusade of Peace—to Vézelay. People from all over Europe followed the call and set off. They carried fourteen heavy wooden crosses to Vézelay as a sign of their desire for peace and reconciliation. At the initiative of French priests,

Ruins of Coventry Cathedral today ▲

German prisoners of war from a nearby camp were also invited to participate. They brought the fifteenth cross, which was listed as a cross of the Germans. Some of the wooden crosses were placed in the cathedral, where they still stand today. Pax Christi continues to be an important peace movement working, in the midst of various conflicts, to bring about peace and reconciliation.

The German-French reconciliation after the Second World War was marked by the conviction that the futility of war after the bitter experiences of the Napoleonic Wars and the two World Wars must not happen again. Many gestures of reconciliation were set, wise and fair contracts were negotiated, youth and art exchange programs were initiated, all of which laid the foundation for a peaceful Europe. Again, the cathedrals were often the symbolic backdrop and framework for the deeper soul healing that was taking place. For example, Konrad Adenauer and Charles de Gaulle visited a peace Mass in Reims at the beginning of German-French reconciliation, while German artist Imi Knöbel was invited to design the new cathedral windows in Reims and Gabrielle Loire from Chartres created the new window in the Wilhelm Memorial Church in Berlin. He used the famous Chartres blue for the big window that almost fills the entire church.

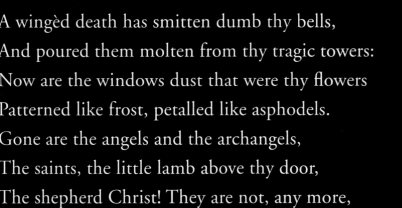

A wingèd death has smitten dumb thy bells,
And poured them molten from thy tragic towers:
Now are the windows dust that were thy flowers
Patterned like frost, petalled like asphodels.
Gone are the angels and the archangels,
The saints, the little lamb above thy door,
The shepherd Christ! They are not, any more,
Save in the soul where exiled beauty dwells.

But who has heard within thy vaulted gloom
That old divine insistence of the sea,
When music flows along the sculptured stone
In tides of prayer, for him thy windows bloom.
Like faithful sunset, warm immortally!
Thy bells live on, and Heaven is in their tone!

—Grace Hazard Conkling,
American poet who lived in France and wrote this poem
about Reims Cathedral in 1914

Window, Reims Cathedral

DESTRUCTION AND
RECONCILIATION

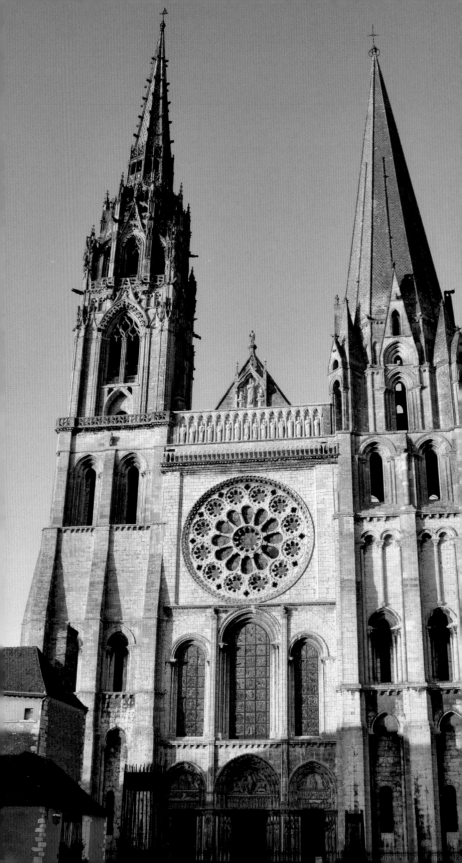

11

CHARTRES CATHEDRAL

Every year at Pentecost, thousands of young people make a pilgrimage from Paris, walking about sixty miles southwest to Chartres, to one of the most beautiful of the Gothic cathedrals. After a couple of days of walking through the fields and forests of France, they catch their first glimpse of the towers of Chartres Cathedral rising majestically in the distant horizon. A day of walking remains, and when the pilgrim finally comes to the valley of the Eure River, one challenge still lies ahead: the old, symbolic 144 pilgrim steps that lead up the hill to the small entrance gate of the village where the first view of the north portal is possible. After just a few more steps forward, the breathtaking cathedral comes into full focus with the towers soaring above, the masterfully crafted stone figures of the north porch extending their welcome, and the mystery of the large rose window crowned by canopies and turrets drawing one's gaze further upward.

Chartres Cathedral is a masterpiece of Gothic design. Amazement meets all who look at and experience this building. It is a library of stone containing a treasure of thousands of years of knowledge. The structure, the interior and outward design, the unique stained glass art, and the relics contained within still impress visitors today.

Chartres has been a holy place since time immemorial. The Celtic druids worshiped there at a sacred spring dedicated to a "pure virgin who will bring the Redeemer." When Christian missionaries reached Chartres around the year 300 CE, the people around Chartres had already turned to Christianity because their

tribal prophecies had been fulfilled. Today the deep well, which dates back to those early Druid times, is located in the lower church.

As early as the fourth century, Chartres became a bishopric, further establishing Christianity in this region. In 876, the diocese received a gift that forever changed its history. King Charles the Bald, the grandson of Charlemagne, bestowed upon the cathedral the Virgin Mary's Veil, which is said to have been what Mary was wearing when the Angel Gabriel announced to her that she would conceive a son. The vast majority of relics found in churches across the world are associated with the death of significant person or saint, and often parts of their bodies that are venerated and honored. But this relic of Mary is associated with her *living*, and it could even have been worn at the time of Jesus's birth. Word spread far and wide of this unique gift's having found a home in Chartres, permanently putting Chartres on the map for attracting pilgrims, beginning in the Middle Ages.

But having "Mary's Shirt" is not the only thing that separates Chartres from other cathedrals. The people of Chartres have long taken seriously that their spectacular cathedral is Mary's earthly home, free for her spirit to enjoy when the doors are locked at the end of each day. To that end, the U-shaped crypt does not have remains of anyone entombed there. It is a house set aside for Mary and no one else. Additionally, Chartres Cathedral is not aligned as usual on the west-east axis. Rather, it is aligned with the moon, whose axis is forty-three degrees to the northeast—the northernmost point of the moonrise. In addition to Mary there are also a surprising number of women who are remembered in stone and glass, including Elizabeth, St. Anne, Bathsheba, Sarah and Hagar, The Queen of Sheba, Mary Magdalene, and a local woman of Chartres, St. Modeste.

By the twelfth century, a large Romanesque church stood in this holy place, succeeding a number of different smaller buildings of previous centuries. But a devastating fire in 1194 destroyed it except for the west facade of the vestibule with its towers and the eleventh-century crypt. Great was the consternation in the population that now the church and

◂ *Nave, Chartres Cathedral*

the Veil were lost. However, during the fire, a couple of sacristans managed to barricade themselves with the veil in the lower church. An iron gate held the burning beam and the molten lead. When the debris was cleared away and the men and the veil were unexpectedly rescued, this was considered a wonder and miracle of Chartres. The grateful town was euphoric and renewed in their belief that they were indeed under the protection of Mary. Citizens joined together and committed to work for three years to rebuild the church. Because of their efforts, the outer building was completed within twenty-six years, therefore becoming the fastest built of the Gothic cathedrals. After the insertion of the windows and figures, the solemn inauguration took place on October 24, 1260. Since then, very little of the structure has changed.

During the French Revolution, the statue of Our Lady of the Virgin, the dark Madonna in the crypt, was burned, and the reliquary shrine with the Veil of Mary was destroyed except for a few remains, which are now kept in two separate reliquaries. However, at this time, when many French cathedrals were ruined, surprisingly little was damaged in Chartres. An amazing 145 of the 186 stained glass windows still have the original glazing from the thirteenth century, more than any other cathedral from this time period.

Currently, a major renovation of the cathedral is taking place. Darkened soot is being removed from the surfaces, to bring it back to a dazzling condition. These restorations are scheduled to be complete in 2026, at which point the cathedral should shine with the same freshness as when first completed.

The wisdom of generations converged in the group of master architects and artisans of Chartres. Concealed within its dimensions, figures, and images, those with eyes to see can find the order of the cosmos and the history of humanity. The focus is on the dignity of humans and their place in the realm of God, with the overarching theme being "God is light." Chartres Cathedral is a festival of light, celebrating life and the supernatural beauty of art and faith.

In many ways female and male energy are balanced in this place. The two different towers, one of the sun, one of the moon, are Chartres's external hallmarks; their dual togetherness and tension continues in the figures and glass windows.

One special feature is the labyrinth embedded in the stone floor of the nave. The labyrinth provides a pilgrim experience in miniature, symbolizing the twists and turns that life often takes. It is a beautiful way to be thoughtful and reflective about one's life, especially when flanked by the stunning stained glass stories of the Old and New Testament on either side. Pilgrims come to walk this path that so many have walked before. In one of the Easter Liturgies, the labyrinth plays a central role when it is lit by candles and one of the priests dances his way through the path into the center while carrying the Easter Candle, celebrating the resurrection of Jesus and the inheritance all people share in this new life. Chartres is one of the most famous of all labyrinth patterns, as well as the most reproduced in the world; copies of it can be found today in a variety of settings on every continent.

Chartres is a powerful place. Many groups travel here to experience the cathedral sometimes for only an hour and others for days at a time. Regardless of the length of time, the opportunity to take in the splendor and vibrant energy that is infused into its very stones often results in its visitors' developing a special relationship with this place that can remain as a source of light for a lifetime. Chartres Cathedral is a gift for the world that strengthens, touches, and inspires all who know it.

"Could Chartres perish? I do not want to believe it. It is waiting for other generations, worthy of understanding her. It waits, proudly lifted from certainty to certainty, testifying to us that, in certain great hours, the human spirit is revived, returns to serene order, tranquility, and creates beauty forever."

—Auguste Rodin,
French sculptor

CHARTRES CATHEDRAL

The labyrinth inside Chartres Cathedral

12

ROSE WINDOWS

Rose windows are often the masterpieces of glasswork in a cathedral. Each one has its own pattern and colors. They are reminders of the circle of life, of the beginning and end of history. Like a great mandala, they symbolize the beauty of God coming to earth and leading humankind to paradise.

They are often divided by the number twelve, the number of the rhythm of time as well as a significant number in biblical history. Twelve is the number of the full circle, a number signifying completion and fulfillment. Sometimes Adam is placed in the center of one of the rose windows, and Jesus faces him on the other side of the church. More often, an image of Mary with the child Jesus on her arm is placed in the center of the rose window in one transept, looking to the rose window in the opposite transept, where Jesus sits in the center, depicting his coming again at the end of time. Frequently, the number theme continues with images that surround the central figure, such as twelve prophets and twelve kings encircling Mary or twenty-four angels or elders surrounding Jesus. The elders often carry musical instruments in their hands, ready to play the great symphony of heaven that is to come.

Representing the rhythm of breath flowing in and out, the main colors are often blue and red. They weave through these spectacular images, bringing them to life and inspiring thoughts of the ever-present give and take moving through one's life. When shadows fall on the windows they become noticeably bluer, and when the sun streams in they become deeper with red. The light makes them seem alive according to the coming and going of the sun.

◀ *Detail, south rose window, Chartres Cathedral*

There are many notable cathedral rose windows that we could mention. Most poignant of all, we think of the beautiful three from Notre-Dame of Paris that survived the awful fire of April 2019. They date back to the thirteenth century.

Rose windows are like letters from paradise. They always shine, though with distinct personality changes as the sun and seasons shift. Sometimes they are quiet and mysterious, sometimes glittering and shiny, sometimes calm and still, sometimes bright and festive, sometimes night blue or daytime red, sometimes silent, sometimes dancing, but always clear and beautiful.

South rose window, as viewed from the north portal, Chartres Cathedral ▲
North rose window, Chartres Cathedral ▶

"All you who seek to honor these doors,
    Marvel not at the gold and expense but at the
    craftsmanship of the work.
The noble work is bright, but, being nobly bright,
    the work
Should brighten the minds, allowing them to travel
    through the lights
To the true light, where Christ is the true door.
    The golden door defines how it is imminent in
    these things.
The dull mind rises to the truth through material
    things,
And is resurrected from its former submersion when
    the light is seen."

—Abbot Suger,
patron of the Church of Saint-Denis,
the first Gothic cathedral

ROSE WINDOWS

◀ *The blue windows, Sagrada Familia*

13

THE CHURCH OF THE TRANSFIGURATION

O verlooking Cape Cod Bay, the Community of Jesus stands on one of the few points on the east coast of the United States where one can observe the sunset over water. A short distance away one can watch the sunrise over the Atlantic Ocean. This natural beginning and end of each day complements well a small community of dedicated people who have chosen to prominently display the Alpha and Omega symbols, representing God who is the beginning and end, in several key places in their recently built church. They are a unique ecumenical community, who combine the teachings of Jesus with Benedictine sensibilities and spirituality, leading to an altogether wholehearted living of the Christian faith. The Rule of Saint Benedict provides inspiration for an inner order; it offers a spiritual path in the search for a meaningful life. The common liturgy, the vow of stability—promising to remain in one's specific community for life—and the willingness to fully bring one's own gifts into this fellowship have led to fascinating and impressive results. It is powerful when like-minded people bind their lives together in faith and Rule.

Begun nearly fifty years ago by two women, Cay Andersen and Judy Sorensen, the Community of Jesus quickly gained momentum and now stands at about two hundred fifty members, including religious sisters and brothers, clergy from a number of different denominations, and lay families. Lay members are responsible for their day jobs and for maintaining personal

◀ *The apse, Church of the Transfiguration*

homes, but they work together to build and take care of their shared community. Out of this sharing of time and talent, along with a strong focus on learning and the arts, the Community has cultivated singing the Liturgy of the Hours in Gregorian Chant, recorded many CDs with their dedicated and well-traveled choir, established a book publishing company, and expanded their housing and community buildings.

Toward the end of the 1900s, the Community began the construction of their glorious Church of the Transfiguration, which brings to physical reality the beliefs they hold dear. To build on the roots of the early and undivided church, they chose the architectural style of "basilica": a nave with low side aisles and a curved apse in the altar area, adorned with Carrara marble, colorful mosaics, and frescoes. One's gaze upon entering is lifted from the tree of life embedded in the floor, to the biblical stories vividly pictured in rows on either side of the nave, to the great wall of the apse where the Risen Christ, whose face incorporates every race, kindly looks on with his arms outstretched over all.

The vision was to give the Church so much attention to detail and rich symbolism that it would be like a living book telling stories of God's presence. Artists were invited to design the different parts. The atrium, bronze doors, capitals, mosaics, frescoes, baptismal font, altar, and glass Transfiguration wall at the western entrance were commissioned by artists from North America and Europe. They, in turn, were expected to work together and train members of the Community, involving them in the construction process. After many years of preparation and thoughtful study and work, the church was dedicated in 2000, and the artwork was completed in 2010.

The Community of Jesus can feel proud of the work they have accomplished together, but what is more impressive to visitors is the hospitality with which they are received upon arrival, as well as their continued mission outreach through a vibrant arts program. In addition to a theater group, a fife and drum corps, a choir, and the various art guilds that developed through the construction of the church, the Community is also still in the process of completing its E. M. Skinner organ. This is no small task, as this instrument will be one of the largest in the world when completed, with 150 ranks and over 12,000 pipes drawn from an eclectic sampling of twenty twentieth-century Skinner organs. The pipes are enclosed along the side aisles of the nave, providing an enormous range of surround-sound listening experiences. Used regularly in worship and in a variety of concerts and demonstrations, the organ symbolizes the heart of this community, as the many sounds and stylings come together in one voice extending into the world.

The atrium, Church of the Transfiguration

Oculus window, Church of the Transfiguration

"Let us make a thing of beauty
That long may live when we are gone;
Let us make a thing of beauty
That hungry souls may feast upon;
Whether it be wood or marble,
Music, art or poetry,
Let us make a thing of beauty
To help set man's bound spirit free."

—Edward Matchett,
British poet and designer

14

SAGRADA FAMILIA

In 1874, when the bookseller Joseph Bocabella had the idea in his hometown of Barcelona to build a church modeled after the Basilica of Loreto, he probably did not suspect what would result from that idea a century and a half later.

Bocabella founded the Society of Friends of St. Joseph and began to collect donations for the purpose of purchasing a large plot on the outskirts of Barcelona. Soon the construction of the crypt began, and it was completed fifteen years later.

True to life, the path for the construction of this great church was anything but straight; rather it resembled a labyrinth characterized by twists and surprising turns. When an unfortunate falling out with the architect occurred and all logical successors were involved in the dispute, a young architect was finally recommended to continue the project: Antonio Gaudí.

Gaudí was born on June 25, 1852, in Reus, Spain. When he was twenty-one, he joined the School of Architecture in Barcelona, where he drew attention because of his revolutionary ideas about imitating nature in his designs for buildings. His professional reputation continued to grow after he undertook larger projects commissioned by the bourgeoisie such as Casa Calvet, Casa Batlló, and Casa Milà. In 1883, he took over the design of Sagrada Familia.

An unplanned turn for the project came in 1894, when an unusually large anonymous donation arrived. This allowed Gaudí to revise his plans and expand considerably. The church building, now a Catholic minor basilica, is to be completed in

2026, and is still financed exclusively by donations. Gaudí worked for 43 years on the cathedral until an unfortunate accident with a tram resulted in his death in 1926.

Gaudí took his inspiration from two sources: the Christian message and nature. One was derived directly from the Holy Scriptures, tradition, and liturgy. The other came from observation of the natural world, providing him with a conceptual and methodological framework. Gaudí did not copy nature but analyzed the function of its elements to formulate structural and formal designs that he then applied to architecture. For example, after a long and careful study of inverted models hung with weights from chains or strings, and graphical calculations, Gaudí arrived at the idea of leaning columns branching out like trees. He employed the idea of a forest, not only as a space of magical lighting conducive to intimacy and meditation, but also as an organized and hierarchical structure for the optimal support of a beautiful vault of leaves.

When finished, the Sagrada Familia will succeed in something that many visionaries have tried before. Several cathedrals across Europe planned for more than just one or two towers, including Reims, which was originally slated for seven, and Chartres, nine; those plans were never fully realized. In its final state, Sagrada will have a staggering total of eighteen, with the main tower being the tallest church tower in the world.

Sagrada Familia is one of the few large-scale church constructions in progress today. With its name, "Holy Family," and its architecture that beautifully captures nature, it is poised to express the central themes of our time. In harmony with its sister cathedrals around the world, it will be a home for the human soul, a shelter through the storms of history yet to come, and a place of inspiration and challenge. It will be a place to look, to wonder, to pray, to celebrate, to reflect, and to rise up emboldened and strengthened to keep family and nature holy.

SAGRADA FAMILIA

"The cathedrals speak the truth that the entirety of the cosmos, from the seraphim to the simplest of elements, form that perfect and complex body which is Christ come to full stature."

—Bishop Robert Barron,
American priest, scholar, and author

The green and blue windows, Sagrada Familia ▶

SAGRADA FAMILIA

15

COLOR
The Coat of Light

The atmosphere within the nave of Sagrada Familia is ripe with awe and wonder with the soaring, nature-inspired ceiling and the rainbow of stained glass on either side. The windows themselves are rather simple in that they do not tell specific Bible stories like those of most other cathedrals. And yet their simplicity should not be underestimated. On a sunny day, light pours through and delivers an experience of color like none other. Vibrant blocks of color permeate the space, the air, and any person standing in its path. This gives one the feeling of being baptized in color, somehow bathed in this penetrating, gentle light of God.

Light is a central theme found in cathedrals everywhere precisely because of its close association with God's Presence. Usually the entrance space of a cathedral is the most dim, symbolizing the darkness of the world. The brightness steadily increases as one moves closer to the altar area. How this specifically plays out is as diverse as the cathedrals themselves—from the clear path of light leading down the center nave aisle of Vézelay Basilica to the array of colors that dance and play on every surface of the Washington National Cathedral or Grace Cathedral in San Francisco. If one is lucky enough to catch an especially bright rising or setting sun in Chartres, the brilliance and intensity of the light streaming through the deep reds and blues of the cathedral's windows give the sense of standing on holy ground. The same can be said about the rays of golden light that float through Michelangelo's dome

◀ *Light on the labyrinth inside Grace Cathedral*

in St. Peter's Basilica down upon the Bernini canopy over the high altar in abundant blessing.

Light is one of the strangest phenomena with which scientists and the human mind grapple. Even though we speak easily of "the speed of light," the concept is barely comprehensible. In one second, light orbits the earth seven times. Light brings unity between Earth and the vast, unimaginable spaces that surround us, and at the same time, light manifests itself in its unpredictability in every corner of our fair planet. Our next neighbor star is four light years away, the nearest galaxy, 2.5 million light years away. Not only does light's speed test the limits of the human brain, but its nature is a mystery that defies explanation. There are description models that can explain individual observations depending on the angle of view. Sometimes light takes on the properties of a particle, which can be explained as something solid, tangible, or materially concrete, but it can also be described as a wave, a vibration that does not carry matter, but energy. Even if quantum physics enables these seemingly incompatible oddities of light to come closer together, light remains a tangible but indeterminable phenomenon.

For every space that people inhabit, we think about how we provide it with light. Often we have electricity, a lamp, and a switch. The more special the room, the more special the light. Light, coloring, incidence of light, shielding and brightening are being considered with ever more sophistication. In sacred spaces, the encounter with light has always been of great importance. In cathedrals, light is a cornerstone of concepts. The design of the shapes, the arrangement of the windows, the importance of colors, the compositions of pictures, and the placement of candles and lamps decisively shape the atmosphere. To be enveloped in a space that opens up to let in light through transparent partitions of windows is like the soul communicating with the universe. In the colorful mosaic patterns of windows, light is transformed, takes on a shape and a color, creates carpets of light on walls, pillars, floors, and on the retinas of our eyes,

◀ *Altar window in St. Peter's Basilica*

and is able to trigger the fascination of how astonishingly beautiful light and its colors can be.

Is light a parable, an expression of God? Is the mysterious, material, or energetic coming from the depths of the universe reaching us? Is one way to get a glimpse of God to say that God is light? Is God the most common energy in the universe, and at the same time an entity that we will never understand?

To witness the light in a cathedral, or a moment when the lighting highlights a particular feature or a special window, is a very special gift. Sometimes the illumination is so fleeting that it can be observed entirely in a few seconds or minutes before the slightest shift changes the scene before one's eyes. It is akin to spying a rare occurrence in nature or catching a spectacular sunset just as the sun hits the surface of the sea. Such instances of transcendence and beauty fortify our faith that God continues to show up and be present. God not only is contained in the stories of the past but also continues to participate in the stories of our lives today.

Inside the Kaiser Wilhelm Gedächtniskirche, Berlin ▶

"Light is not simply a functional brightness that clears space for visibility. Perhaps of all the elements, light has the most refined imagination; it is never merely a medium. Light is the greatest unnoticed force of transfiguration in the world: it literally alters everything it touches and through color dresses nature to delight, befriend, inspire and shelter us."

—John O'Donohue,
Irish poet and priest

▲ *Blue Virgin window, Chartres Cathedral*

Colors dancing on the pillars of Washington National Cathedral ▶

COLOR
The Coat of Light

16

ELY CATHEDRAL

Because of the especially dramatic sequence of events in England during the reign of King Henry VIII at the time of the Reformation in the sixteenth century, followed by the short-lived and particularly destructive Commonwealth of Oliver Cromwell, it is not unusual to see the outer shells of destroyed churches and monasteries still dotting the landscape of the British Isles. The effort to eradicate anything resembling Catholicism was, at times, swift and brutal, with relics, icons, statues, and stained glass quickly being reduced to rubble. For buildings that did survive this time period, there is often evidence that they were affected in that statues were defaced or removed altogether, leaving empty bays where they once stood. Such is the case with Ely Cathedral. It managed to escape relatively unscathed, perhaps because Oliver Cromwell lived in Ely for several years and had at least a distant connection with its cathedral.

The origin of this extraordinary space stretches back to the late seventh century, when a monastery was founded in Ely by the Norman queen and the first abbess, Etheldreda. Located among the fields of southeast England, the spot was somewhat secluded for a religious community, as it was tucked into a small settlement. Following the success of Etheldreda's monastery, however, it was destroyed a couple of centuries later by a group of Danes and then re-established in the tenth century by a Benedictine community. The architectural history of today's Ely Cathedral—what was once the abbey church and then part

The Octagon, Ely Cathedral

of the Church of England during the Reformation—spans from the eleventh century to the present day, with the nave being erected in the twelfth century and the aisles and choir in the thirteenth.

English Gothic architecture developed its own style called "decorated." Foliage, loop decorations, arches, and colorful painting of the church characterize it. Ely Cathedral is known for this, with a particular fineness and joy of color.

Catastrophe struck in the early fourteenth century when the central tower collapsed due to insufficient support. The religious community was given the unexpected opportunity to dream and realize a new vision for the space, and they certainly rose to the occasion! The new dome would be in the form of an octagon, a common shape used to symbolize eternity. Sometimes this is described in terms of the "eighth day," where heaven and earth meet in the day beyond earthly structured time. But the brilliance, grace, and illuminated beauty of this dome design is decidedly uncommon and has resulted in a vault that is one of the most impressive of its kind. Sixteen particularly long and straight oak trunks were required for the timber construction. For this purpose, a separate commission was established, and the search began through the forests to find just the right ones needed.

The West Tower, standing over the vestibule, was executed without intermediate ceilings so that you can look up to a picture of Christ about sixty-three meters, or 206 feet, above. A labyrinth is incorporated into the floor underneath, with the length of its path also measuring sixty-three meters, or 206 feet. Visitors can walk it imagining the path as moving toward Jesus.

ELY CATHEDRAL

The parish community of the cathedral made the decision to commission three pieces of art as a way to continue to tell their story of faith into the new millennium. One is a vibrant statue of Mary having just received the news from Gabriel of a coming baby, another is a sculpture of Jesus that is positioned above the pulpit, and the third sculpture is a large-scale cross, entitled "The Way of Life," that looms above the labyrinth on the north wall. The bottom portion of this cross extends in a zigzagged and curved path down the wall, which is in relative darkness. A light illuminates the cross at the top. Within this one image, visitors can imagine themselves at various points in life on that twisted Way while realizing that the curve in the darkness is not the final answer. Light and Life are connected to the path even if not visible from every point. That this sculpture is hovering above the labyrinth only deepens the rich symbolism of how strange and unexpected, and yet secure, the single path toward the center can be.

Throughout its eventful history, Ely Cathedral has been a beacon of light in this quiet corner of the world. The stories it continues to proclaim through music, art, and the open hearts of the community are a gift to all who enter.

Ely Cathedral

"'Let us respond to disaster,' they might have said to themselves, 'by founding our design upon the number eight which signifies regeneration, the new life, and the just balance between the powers of the spirit and the powers of nature. . . . Let us create something new that will be stronger than the tower it replaces and yet will seem more daring, more dangerous, more thrilling than anything ever built before. Let us astound the future.'"

—William Anderson,
Scottish painter and writer

ELY CATHEDRAL

17

GRACE CATHEDRAL

It was considered a special grace, especially for pioneers, to have made the long journey safely across the North American continent to the Pacific. Such was the name of the small Episcopal church at Nob Hill in San Francisco: Grace Church. All further extensions retained this name as the church began to grow larger.

In the great earthquake of 1906, the subsequent fires destroyed large parts of the city of San Francisco, including Grace Church. The dramatic ruin became a national symbol of the disaster. In the reconstruction, earthquake resistance was a major topic, and reinforced steel concrete construction was chosen with which to build a new cathedral in neo-Gothic style. During the economic crisis of the 1930s construction had to be stopped, even though it was already well advanced. The last four bays of the nave were completed in the early 1960s. One easily notices the change from the old to the new style of stained glass windows within the nave. In 1964, the finished church was consecrated.

Meanwhile, Grace Cathedral was in the midst of the social upheaval of that turbulent decade. It was already its custom to welcome all, but when neighborhood hippies began to show up in large numbers, often causing disruptions to ecclesial activity, they challenged the commitment of the cathedral to remain open. In fact, this long-standing faith community already reflected the colorful, diverse life of its bubbling young city, circling all the way back to the builders' vision, which included

uniquely themed windows and mapping out part of the crypt for use as meeting rooms. Similarly, the upper clerestory windows were not occupied with traditional saints, but with people in history who have advanced humanity in some way. Albert Einstein and John Glenn are the first on either side of these nave windows that portray the endeavors of humanity. The last in the series, which is also the newest in the church, is a spiral galaxy representing both the cosmos at large and within.

The tradition of radical hospitality—being a sanctuary house of prayer within a sanctuary city—with a keen awareness of the burning issues of each generation, continues to this day. At the height of the AIDS crisis, an interdenominational chapel was built for victims, including an altarpiece that was the last work by Keith Haring before his death. Multiple AIDS quilts commemorate beloved victims of humanity's greatest twentieth-century plague.

Most recently, a new altar for gun victims has been set up, where every week a picture of an innocent victim is shown. The focal point is a thought-provoking Madonna icon, where both Mary and Jesus (encircled in her womb) have their arms raised in a "don't shoot" position; even more poignant, the cross that covers Jesus is also a target. Grace Cathedral does not sit on the sidelines of culture, but actively participates, albeit sometimes uncomfortably, in the middle of surrounding social and political arenas. This remains a core value of the church.

Against the backdrop of this diversity and activity, the love of liturgy and music are essentials of this place. This ranges from Bobby McFerrin's offering to help organize and sing for twenty-four hours of healing chant on New Year's Eve to the church choirs' filling the house with glorious sacred choral singing throughout the week.

A special feature of Grace Cathedral, like Chartres, is its labyrinth, which was first introduced in 1991 and is now permanently installed in the floor of the nave. It is the same shape and size as the one in Chartres. The labyrinth as a place of contemplation of one's

◄ *Rose window, Grace Cathedral*

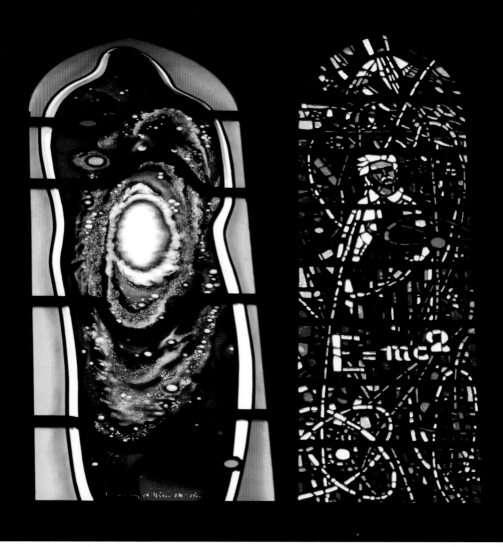

own personal experiences was initially viewed skeptically, but the appreciation of the people soon convinced the community that it offers fertile ground for those who are seeking. Events, services, candle walks, and meditations are now held regularly on the labyrinth, making this church, for some, a pilgrim destination. The deep breaths many take at the center of the labyrinth add to the warmth of this place, filling it with new life and stories under the shades of grace.

△ *Windows, Grace Cathedral*
The Interfaith AIDS Memorial Chapel with an altar piece by Keith Haring, Grace Cathedral ▷

"Since we cannot prolong life,
we have to condense it."

—Roger Willemsen,
German author and television presenter

GRACE CATHEDRAL

18

NOTRE-DAME BASILICA

When Notre-Dame Basilica in Montréal was finished in 1829, it remained the largest church on the continent for fifty years, holding as many as 3,000 people for worship. Sainte-Chapelle in Paris was the inspiration for the architecture of this church, with its fine columns, elegant lines, a special painting of the interior, and an impressive staging of the light. A blue starry sky, consisting not only of stars but also of the lilies of the French royal family, gives the whole space the magical feeling of being under an open sky. From niches and windows light shines forth, as though from welcoming little houses in the middle of a dark night. The delicate arches carry the vaults like trees that nestle against a roof. The light inlets arranged in the ceiling are like large mandalas forming a transparent curtain. The painted pillars complete the impression of entering a fairytale, and the visitor is enraptured by this "other" world upon passing through the doors. Looking to the backside of the entrance wall, the visitor beholds a beautifully arranged pipe organ, one of the largest and oldest in all North America. The entire setting of the room elicits a fervent "wow," even from eyes spoiled by today's standards of stage settings and film illusions.

Recently, the basilica staff had the idea of adding further to the impressive room with a light show. Unlike a number of European cities that have developed light shows on the outside facade of their cathedrals, the people of Montréal chose to highlight the exquisite details of the inside. In doing so they have achieved particular success. The "wow" factor is significantly increased when this holy space is viewed through this highlighted lens.

◀ *Altar in Notre-Dame Basilica, Montréal*

When worship is celebrated in this magnificent space, the Word of God takes on a special meaning. Its task is to bring the worshipers to the ground of reality, as do the unpainted expressive wooden figures that stand in the niches or under the pulpit. They represent the cornerstones of prophecy and preaching and provoke all to make a stand in our time as prophets and preachers.

Those who find themselves in the sanctuary that houses the Sacred Heart Chapel, which was reestablished in 1987 after a fire, can see that this space anticipates the challenges of our time. The artist of the bronze altar wall, Charles Doudelin, puts it this way: "I had one goal in mind: to touch the mural, not just as a sculpture, but in the spiritual sense of the word." It is worth pausing and turning the external impression to the silence of the interior, asking the question: What will happen to our beautiful and yet brutal world?

This strikingly beautiful basilica serves as a pivot point in the heart of the city, where it compels passersby to be more open to the movement of the Divine in their midst in ways large and small. It inspires willing souls, and the tender image of being wrapped in its blue starry mantle remains with the visitor long after leaving the warmth of this shelter. Standing outside the basilica today, one may be overshadowed by Montréal's towering office buildings, but the church as a product of nineteenth-century Romanticism remains a symbol of faith and values that inspired the founders of Montréal and its inhabitants. To this day, it continues to be a living memory and the soul of Montréal.

"Bear in mind that you are not building a temporary structure, but I assure you that the history of your edifice shall be transmitted to future generations."

—James O'Donnell,
architect of Notre-Dame in Montréal

The New Chapel, Notre-Dame Basilica, Montréal ▶

Debout!
Veillons

NOTRE-DAME BASILICA

19

INCLINE THE EAR OF YOUR HEART

W hen Mary was pregnant with Jesus, the Gospel tells us that she stayed for a time with her relative Elizabeth, who was also with child. Given the unique and powerful circumstances these women found themselves in, they must have found much solace, comfort, and affection in each other's company. We imagine them literally leaning into each other, and this inclination is sensitively expressed in many cathedrals, especially in portal figures and stained glass in Chartres.

A cathedral is a place of listening; a dome of silence and contemplation envelops us. In this space, our senses adjust, and the inner ear aligns with the near-palpable pulse of the Eternal. In one image at Chartres Cathedral, Mary is even shown holding her hand to her ear as the shepherds tell her what they have experienced in the field. This is an insightful way to portray the words of the Gospel of Luke, "She pondered all these things in her heart." In another portal depicting the resurrection of Jesus, the disciples stretch their ears to heaven to hear what is said and sung in that moment.

The Rule of Saint Benedict, the basic rule of many great monastic orders, begins with the words: "Incline the ear of your heart." Not only do we possess external ears, but we obviously have a finely tuned internal way to perceive things that are not spoken or seen. Inclining the ear of our heart is the invitation to hear the voice of God, to internalize the angels' oft-repeated message to "Be not afraid," to lean toward each other and hear what goes beyond words. Inclining the ear of our heart is the invitation to respond to what we hear and anticipate.

Mary and Elizabeth, Chartres Cathedral ▶

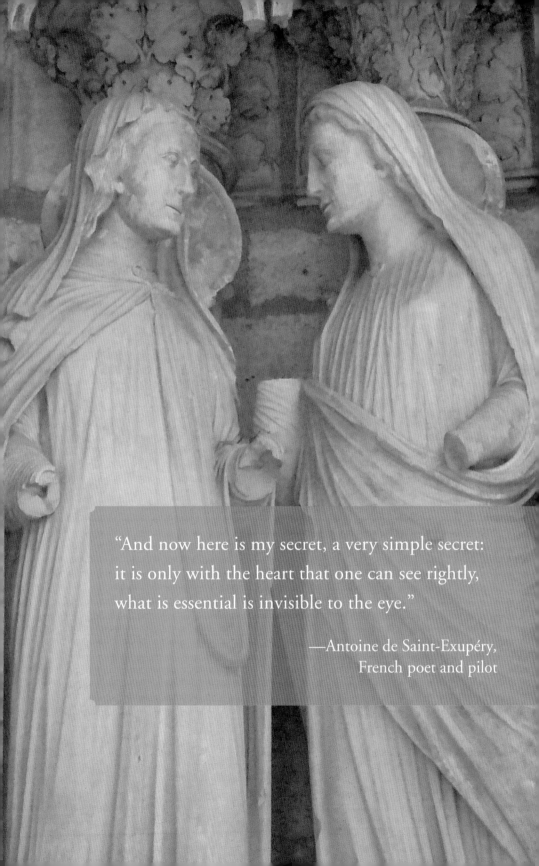

"And now here is my secret, a very simple secret: it is only with the heart that one can see rightly, what is essential is invisible to the eye."

—Antoine de Saint-Exupéry, French poet and pilot

20

THE CATHEDRAL OF
ST. JOHN THE DIVINE

I n the history of cathedrals one reads again and again of
devastating fires. This book was written when Notre-Dame
of Paris had recently experienced a fire that nearly destroyed
what had stood so beautifully since the twelfth century. The
heat of a fire sometimes makes the stones so brittle and fragile
that they lose their capacity to provide sound support, and the
cathedral has to be demolished and rebuilt. Sometimes a fire
only destroys windows and the chemise stones. Every fire is a
disaster, because it is difficult to raise the money for rebuilding
and once again gather all the forces of hope and vision to build
the cathedral over many years.

When a wing of the Cathedral Church of St. John the Divine
erupted in flames on December 18, 2001, a week before
thousands were to gather for its late Christmas Eve service, the
intense heat shattered several stained glass windows, and orange
towers of fire leapt forty feet in the air, filling the cavernous
sanctuary from floor to vaulted ceiling with smoke. The fire
had started in the gift shop, possibly in a waste basket. Due
to modern means of firefighting, it was brought under control
after several hours. Still, left in the ashes was a devastated site.

Located on Amsterdam Avenue in Manhattan, St. John the
Divine is America's largest cathedral and the principal church
of the Episcopal Diocese of New York. Its cornerstone was laid
in 1892, but the cathedral remains unfinished. Construction of
the north transept, where the fire began, was stopped in 1941.

When a visitor enters the cathedral today its grandeur and bright nave give an initial feeling of enormity. The southern rose window, with a dark-skinned Jesus in its center, falls in line with the great rose windows of cathedrals in France. Like a bright blue blossom, it is as if it were a door into heaven. If you look to the transept, both the history of not being able to finish the church and the soot of the great fire give it the appearance of a deep, black hole. However, beyond the depths there are hints of gold shimmering light coming from the apse.

A unique piece of art, installed in 2015 by artist Tom Otterness, frames the darkness. In the servant columns of the large supporting arch surrounding the entrance of the transept, every second stone was taken out. In the interspaces sit small stone figures like oddly shaped round dolls accompanied by all sorts of symbols, such as fish and dollar signs. In the heart of this vast church at the seam where the light and darkness meet, this art installation is appropriately named "Life and Death."

The church is currently undergoing renovations, not in the area damaged by fire, but in the vault of the nave. The darkness and incompleteness of the transept has an atmosphere of sadness, but at the same time it leads one's thoughts to the great words "I do not forsake you." In the midst of the darkness, the altar table remains steadfast with the ever-hopeful invitation to celebrate the Resurrection. Thus, this cathedral speaks its own language—the symbolism; the strong contrast between light, dark, and semi-dark; radiant beauty and gloominess; and idiosyncratic art, with its unusual questions—that resonates powerfully in a city of such diversity.

New York City, as few other cities can understand, is a place in which light and dark, rich and poor, grand and miserable, and people from all the corners of the world live, breathe, and move in tight geographic confines. St. John the Divine stands its ground there and tells a story that reflects not only the image of its city, but

Tom Otterness artwork in the column of St. John the Divine

also the whole world. The caretakers of the cathedral try to make it a house of peace, inviting prophetic and eloquent leaders such as Dr. Martin Luther King, Nelson Mandela, and H.H. the Dalai Lama to be guests and speak to the people. Also, music and art play an important role, as is often the case with cathedrals, to strengthen the joy of undertaking this human pilgrimage on earth, all united under the same dark sky and the endless shining sun.

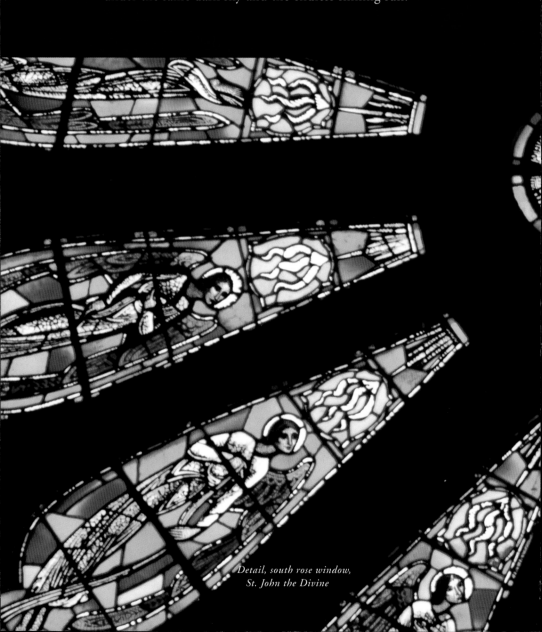

Detail, south rose window,
St. John the Divine

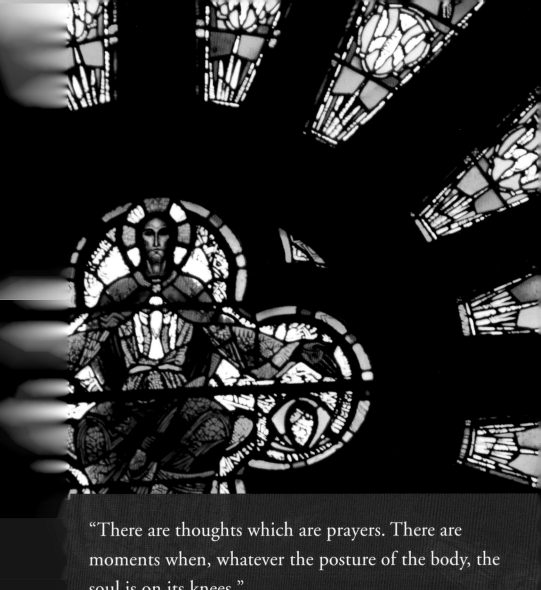

"There are thoughts which are prayers. There are moments when, whatever the posture of the body, the soul is on its knees."

—Victor Hugo,
French novelist

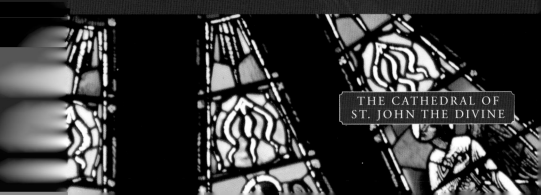

THE CATHEDRAL OF
ST. JOHN THE DIVINE

21

THE CATHEDRAL AS MUSIC

From the outside, cathedrals are monumental witnesses of the yearning of humankind for order and harmony. Wherever your gaze wanders, from the facades with their gantries and towers to the artful buttresses with their recurring forms of arches, piers, and pillars, you find rhythm. This feeling increases even more when you enter the interior. You find a whole symphony of forms and rhythms, a game of condensation and dissolution into which you are taken. Although each cathedral has its own laws in the arrangement of the main and side aisles with their different number of arcades, there is a common thread that connects them. The master builders and artists of each one saw themselves as earthly representatives of the Builder, God, who created the world according to certain laws. "But you have arranged everything according to measure, number and weight," says the Book of Wisdom.

And so master builders studied the rhythms, proportions, and forms of creation and the cosmos in order to repeat them in the construction of their cathedrals, as though they were some kind of cosmic mirror. That is why the fascination for cathedrals has lasted through the ages to the present day, because there were people at work who wanted to experience nothing less than a "paradisiacal order" on earth. If one lets this built-up order of architecture seep into the soul, the concept of universal and timeless structures can rise within us even today. At such moments, resonance is struck between us and the ancient cathedral at which we gaze, which then becomes less museumlike and more like an exquisite piece of music that never stops being played. It is as though we have woken up, or, as the German poet Joseph Eichendorff put it:

Sleeps a song in things abounding,
that keep dreaming to be heard,
Earth's tunes will start resounding,
if you find the magic word.

If one follows the poetic picture of the magic word and asks for the basic starting point of all these resonating vibrational phenomena and ordering principles, one ends up with two things: numbers and words. In the imagination of the Middle Ages, the Divine revealed itself through number and word into visible reality. The range of subjects of the various cathedral schools, therefore, consisted of word and number sciences, to which music also belonged. Music was understood and taught comprehensively—including *musica instrumentalis*, learning an instrument; *musica humana*, knowledge of the rhythms and proportions of human beings; and *musica mundana*, the harmonic structure of the world.

This harmonious understanding of the world was the fundamental principle of the Gothic master builders, which is why cathedral architecture was based so much on numbers and musical proportions, so much so that we may even call it "built music." Everywhere you will find in the construction of a cathedral thirds, fourths, and fifths, which act as mirrors or resonance chambers to all the sounds within.

If you are fortunate enough to hear real music in a cathedral, you will be able to experience in a fascinating way how the building plays along, carries the sounds through the room, and lets it resonate in the vaults. In such moments, you can hear the wisdom of the builders, who, drawing on the spiritual order of the cosmos, built these symphonies of stone and glass, rhythm and sound for the generations to come.

Choir, Chartres Cathedral

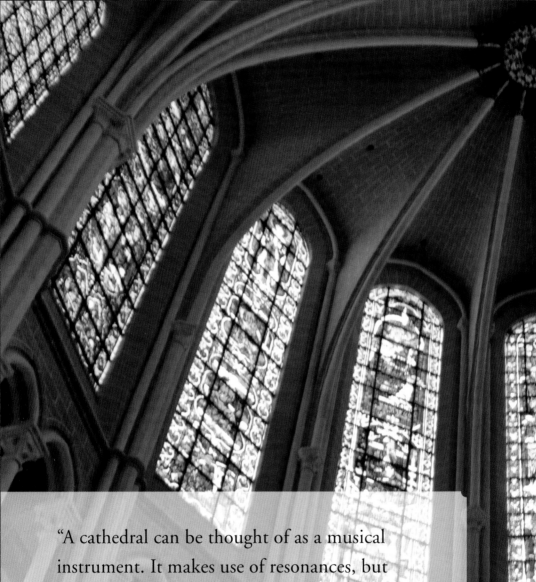

"A cathedral can be thought of as a musical instrument. It makes use of resonances, but the principal part is the emptiness. The master craftsman tunes the emptiness in the quality, volume and tension of the stone."

—Paula D'Arcy,
American author

THE CATHEDRAL
AS MUSIC

Ulm Minster

22

ULM MINSTER

The foundation stone of the Ulm Minster (from the German *Ulmer Münster*) church was laid in 1377. But it was only in the nineteenth century that the tower was built according to the old plans, thus implementing the idea of a harmoniously proportioned Gothic church. The last stone, the finial at the top of the church tower, was placed in 1890. Thus, the tower of Ulm Minster, 161 meters (528 feet) high, became the highest church tower in the world.

Since the tower is not beside the church but rather integrated into the nave, a tower hall connects behind the entrance gate. From the middle of the tower hall you can see the top of the tower through an open rosette next to the bells. However, this unique view is rarely possible because the damper is usually closed for safety reasons. The inserted tower grows upward and makes the church an impressive building striving for the sky. Like a beacon of hope, a guardian of freedom and peace, and its own inner pursuit of a strong and sincere faith, Ulm Minster is a true skyscraper.

Inside there is an artistically carved choir stall that stands out not only for its quality, but also for its remarkable commitment to an open mind. Famous men of antiquity, such as Virgil, Cicero, and Seneca face the prophetic women, the Sibyls. This expresses the necessary balance between mind and soul, knowledge and intuition, experience and vision. It creates a dynamic space within which to pray and sing to the glory of the creator of such a diverse world.

In 1530, a referendum found a majority of Ulm citizens favored a switch to the Protestant faith, and so what was a Catholic cathedral is today the largest Protestant church in Germany.

The beautiful Gothic stone carving artwork of the sound board above the pulpit has a unique symbolism that is able to conjure a smile in the viewer. When you look closely, you see a small spiral staircase inside. It leads to a second smaller pulpit that is far too small for a person to climb. Here the hidden preacher, the Holy Spirit, speaks. He is the one to change the listener's soul.

The stained glass windows in the south and north nave aisles were completely destroyed during World War II. After the war, the gaps were filled with plain glass. In the course of time they were replaced by modern windows designed by famous artists. Two of them, designed by Johannes Schreiter, are called "World Endangered" and "World Completed." In their clear structures they express the seriousness of our responsibility for the world, but also God's control over all of time. Right beside them the Israel window with the names of the concentration camps Treblinka, Auschwitz, and Bergen-Belsen written at the bottom remind us that we never should ever forget what happened there.

A figure of Jesus, the Man of Sorrow, is one of the most famous sculptures of Ulm. Jesus still bears the marks of pain in his face, but he stands in a gracious way, turning to the people. He is the master of vulnerability and grace, standing with us.

"I never weary of great churches. It is my favorite kind of mountain scenery. Mankind was never so happily inspired as when it made a cathedral."

—Robert Louis Stevenson,
Scottish novelist and travel writer

ULM MINSTER

23

ST PATRICK'S CATHEDRAL

For well over a century, St. Patrick's Cathedral has stood in the middle of Manhattan Island, a beacon for many. It now overlooks extravagant 5th Avenue and Rockefeller Center and seems to be dwarfed by its neighboring buildings. Landscapes change over time, but the archbishop who birthed the vision that the church should stand in this exact place was nearly laughed off the island when he dared to suggest its location be in such a remote location related to the city in his day.

New York City has welcomed millions of immigrants over the centuries, her harbor and the Statue of Liberty receiving the tired and weary but grateful people making their path to a new land where the promise of freedom rings. Archbishop John Hughes, who himself arrived in New York as an immigrant from Ireland, wanted St. Patrick's to be a place of beauty and hope, always up to the task of meeting whatever need arose in this bustling and growing city.

Manhattan is a classic city of urban canyons. Skyscrapers line up closely and form seemingly endless walls between which traffic and people move. At the time of its completion in 1878, St. Patrick's Cathedral was an impressive building on the outskirts of New York, but today it is wedged between rows of high-rises. Like a message of progress, the city symbolizes the overwhelming magnitude and power of the world and its need for expansion and influence. The cathedral is surrounded by the demands of money, economics, and the pursuit of power and influence. From across the street a bronze statue of the ancient Greek god Atlas stands in direct view of the church's large front doors. One cannot be sure whether he will soon go to his knees under the weight of the earth he carries or will be able to balance it on his shoulders for a long time.

Moving from the noisy street to the inside of the great cathedral, one embraces the familiar and facilitating silence of a house of God. Freshly renovated, it radiates a natural and unobtrusive calm that leads to the other parts of life that stand in opposition to the quest for wealth and success.

In addition to the tidy and clear overall impression in St. Patrick, small details were deliberately set to lead the visitor to the other side of human reality. In the side altars are figures and images of people who, in their dedication and determination, have given their lives to selfless service to others. A bronze figure of Mother Teresa, sunken in prayer, stands out strikingly. There is also an image of the great Pietà, who here and elsewhere is reminiscent of the original pain of humans, that there is none greater than holding your own dead child in your arms. Continuing around the apse, other saints are highlighted, such as Elizabeth Ann Bayley Seton, who founded the first American congregation of religious sisters, the Sisters of Charity. Or, Charbel Makhlouf, a Maronite monk and priest from Lebanon, as well as a picture of Mary as Our Lady of Guadalupe, who has a touching influence on the people of the American continents. Her consolation, her loving message, has led to amazing changes in people and culture that have influenced the history of the Americas.

St. Patrick's is visited by five million people of every race and creed each year. Thankful immigrants continue to make their offerings for safe passage or to offer their prayers for others' difficult journeys. A number of flower bouquets can be found under the watchful and loving eye of the image of Our Lady of Guadalupe, often given in gratitude for another safe crossing of the border. The cathedral has remained the spiritual center of downtown New York. No matter how big the environment has become and may be, the message of this church remains embedded in this place: that the true greatness of humans is found in inner and selfless tasks, through God's grace.

Nave, St. Patrick's Cathedral ▶

"I pray to God to give me perseverance and to deign that I be a faithful witness to Him to the end of my life."

—St. Patrick,
missionary to Ireland

ST. PATRICK'S
CATHEDRAL

24

CATHEDRAL OF SANTIAGO DE COMPOSTELA

Pilgrims have been traveling on sacred roads since time immemorial. Some historians suggest that since the Bronze Age important pilgrimage routes in Europe led to the extreme west, toward the setting sun. This place was thought to be the closest to the Promised Land that lies behind the sea, which also parallels the metaphoric land that is reached at the setting sun of each life. These trails end in France and Spain on the westernmost headlands to the Atlantic. The points where the continent comes to an end are called *Finis Terra*—the End of the World.

Not far from *Finis Terra* in Spain, in the year 814 the hermit Pelagius saw in the night sky strange apparitions that eventually led him to a field where he rediscovered the forgotten grave of the Apostle James. At this place, called *compostela* from a Latin root meaning *starry field*, a church was built that later became a cathedral. St. James's grave became a pilgrim site that continues to draw thousands of people from all of Europe, and indeed from all around the world, to this place. So many people have traveled to this point through the centuries that paths and trails have been created from many distant places beyond Spain. Most pilgrims today walk at least the last 250 kilometers (155 miles) from any number of starting points.

The Cathedral of Santiago de Compostela rises above a square forecourt. The construction was started in 1075 and completed in 1211. Since then much reconstruction work has been done, changing each time according to current tastes and styles. Today, the cathedral is a thoroughly successful blend of Romanesque, Gothic, Baroque, and Classical elements.

Protected in an enclosed narthex is the Pórtico de la Gloria, the royal portal into the church. Surrounding this grand entrance are joyful stone figures that are sculptural masterpieces from the twelfth century. With their friendly faces, they seem to extend an invitation to a celebration, and indeed, when pilgrims reach this threshold after days, weeks, or months of walking, they want to celebrate that arrival. Several places within the entrance space have become literal touchstones—places where pilgrims and visitors may physically touch what they have been longing to reach for so long.

In the central column of the Pórtico de la Gloria is a statue of the Apostle James, and under him the Root of Jesse, represented by a marble tree. For centuries, pilgrims have touched the tree, and a handprint has become visible in the soft stone. Likewise, there is a staircase behind the figure of St. James in the high altar area, and one can climb up and lay hands on the apostle's shoulders. All pilgrims who have walked more than 100 kilometers, or 62 miles (cyclists 200 kilometers or 124 miles) to Santiago receive an entry in the Pilgrims' Book of the Cathedral and a certificate. This book is now a historic treasure because it documents the names of so many pilgrims, spanning centuries.

A foretaste of the open vaults and marching columns down the nave of the Pórtico de la Gloria can be glimpsed through the doors. The stonemason of the delightful portal figures framing this view was Master Mateo, who is still seen today as a model of stonemasons. At the foot of the central column on the inside looking toward the main altar of the cathedral one finds the small kneeling figure of Mateo himself holding a sign on which is written *Architectus*. This image is popularly known as Santo dos Croques, or "Saint of the Bumps," from the ancient tradition of students hitting their heads against the figure for wisdom, a tradition that was adopted later

Two kingly musicians, Pórtico de la Gloria, Santiago de Compostela ▶

by pilgrims, although steps are being taken to limit access to this well-worn figure to stem the deterioration from which the work has suffered.

Another special feature of this cathedral is its oversized censer, a vessel for burning incense, known as the Botafumeiro. On high holidays, or on order, the famous Botafumeiro is swung in the transept. Five feet tall and hanging from a thirty-meter (ninety-eight-foot) rope, the mighty censer is set in motion by eight people and swung high under the ceiling. Apart from its usual function in the liturgy, the Botafumeiro probably also served to neutralize the smell of the pilgrims, who after their pilgrimage on the Way of St. James would traditionally spend an entire night in prayer and silence in the cathedral.

In recent years, pilgrimages in Europe and around the world seem to be reviving. Half of the pilgrims coming to Santiago are from Spain, followed by pilgrims from Italy, Germany, the USA, and Portugal. There are also many pilgrims from Korea, Canada, and Mexico.

In Spain, France, and Germany, but also widely branching into the far reaches of the European continent, all the paths forming part of the Way of St. James were signposted in recent years. This has resulted in a network of marked trails along which pilgrim hostels have emerged to accommodate the wave of pilgrims who continue to be compelled toward *Finis Terra*.

Statue of Jacob the Elder, Santiago de Compostela ▶

"There is one great truth on this planet: whoever you are, or whatever it is that you do, when you really want something, it's because that desire originated in the soul of the universe."

—Paulo Coelho,
Brazilian novelist

CATHEDRAL OF
SANTIAGO DE COMPOSTELA

In the fields near Chartres

25

PILGRIMAGE

People of all times and tribes have made pilgrimages to holy places, holy images, holy people, or to *finis terra*, the end of the world. Pilgrimage is about tracing essential elements of life: breaking away from what is "normal," progressing with patience and perseverance, finding companions, experiencing fellowship, seeking and finding the sacred, arriving, standing, gathering insights, and then, strengthened by the wealth of experience gained, setting out for the return home.

Depending on the mode of transportation and the distance to the site, some pilgrimages can take weeks and months, while smaller pilgrimage destinations can often be reached on a day trip. Temples, churches, and cathedrals have often been built on ancient holy sites or to house a precious relic, which makes the anticipated arrival that much more special.

In the Christian European tradition in the West, three major pilgrimage destinations have emerged: the Church of the Holy Sepulcher in Jerusalem, St. Peter's Basilica in Rome, and the Cathedral of Santiago de Compostela described in the preceding chapter. In North America, the greatest pilgrimage site is to the Basilica of Our Lady of Guadalupe in Mexico City.

For most of history, the primary mode of travel for pilgrims was walking, with the height of this activity happening during the Middle Ages. Still today people often deliberately choose to walk.

While most people today no longer take a solemn vow before going on pilgrimage, as our medieval counterparts did, the essence of the desire for a transformational experience remains alive and well. Many pilgrims make plans to walk long distances to arrive in a holy place. However, it is equally true that many others no longer spend days hiking, but they travel as tourists and visit the pilgrimage destination for only a short time. They too are pilgrims, of a different but related sort, who want to see the special place, feel its magic, experience its art, and capture the most impressive elements in photos to take back home as a reminder of the special experience.

For all, when the destination is reached, the second and equally important step of every pilgrimage is the way home. The time then comes no longer to turn one's eyes toward the holy place and an encounter with God, but toward one's own home, family, and neighbors, and toward the task of translating the pilgrimage experience into everyday life. If a pilgrim succeeds in weaving impressions from the place of power and holiness into the innermost being and the work of regular life, then this person will be stronger and more beautiful and inspired.

The following prayer has accompanied pilgrims for centuries: "All pilgrims in the world know three steps of the pilgrimage: humility, trust, and compassion. May I reach the goal, and the path shall lead me home."

"144 Steps to Glory"—the entrance for pilgrims, Chartres ▶

"As a form of devotion that engaged the entire being—the body as well as the spirit—the pilgrimage removed from his familiar environment the person who had decided to endure the difficulties and suffering of the road in order to be sanctified. Exiled, a stranger to those he met, the pilgrim's long march was a form of asceticism and penitence, aiming for purification and salvation of the soul, perfected by the contact with holy places."

—Julie Roux,
French historian

PILGRIMAGE

26

BASILICA OF OUR LADY
OF GUADALUPE

Some people may be surprised to hear that there is a pilgrimage destination that draws three or four times as many people as Mecca does each year. Or put another way, if one asks what is the most-visited church in the world, there is one place which puts Notre-Dame in Paris and St. Peter's in Vatican City down a notch on the list: the Basilica of Our Lady of Guadalupe in Mexico City. Each year it is believed that twenty million people visit the basilica, and nine million of those come for the Virgin of Guadalupe's feast day on December 12. The story behind this place is full of wonders and other astonishing tales from its beginning until today.

After the arrival of the Spanish conquistadors in 1519, there was at first curiosity and awe between the highly developed indigenous cultures and the bearded whites, but soon the polytheistic Aztecs, the largest tribe in Mexico, and the Spaniards became enemies. By 1521, Spain was in charge over central Mexico, resulting in dramatic changes within the classes of Aztec society, including forbidding the worship of pagan gods. Within a short period of time, the native people had witnessed thousands of their own die due to rampant disease, they had seen their entire societal structure dismantled, and they were also experiencing their own crisis of faith. Spanish missionaries were sent to convert these natives in the early years following the Aztecs' defeat, but they were met with dismal success, their old methods of proselytizing not proving effective.

◀ *The miraculous image of Our Lady of Guadalupe*

Toribio de Benavente, OFM, one of the first Spanish missionaries in Mexico and a member of the historic 1524 dialogue with Aztec priests and nobles, wrote in his diary: "According to human belief, there is no possibility for them to be open to Christianity unless God does a miracle."

But then, this miracle indeed happened, and within a few years, more than eight million Aztecs wanted to be baptized. What led to this unique wave of conversion? On December 9, 1531, an indigenous man named Juan Diego began walking early to participate in a service in the little church of Tlatelolco, situated behind a hill. Juan Diego was one of the few early Aztec converts to the Christian faith. As he approached Tepeyac Hill, he suddenly heard the voice of a woman speaking to him in his mother tongue saying: "Juanito, my dearest little son, I will help, I will listen to your tears and your troubles and relieve your suffering. Go to the bishop of the city of Mexico and tell him that I have sent you, with the task to build a church here on this hill." Juan made his way to the bishop, who was skeptical and sent the simple native away. As the story goes, Juan was visited by the woman several more times and finally asked to collect flowers on the hillside into his *tilma*, a simple cloak woven from cactus fiber, and to take them to the bishop. As Juan Diego opened his tilma, the flowers fell to the floor, revealing a beautiful image of the woman on its fabric. Impressed by this miracle, the bishop repented for not believing Juan and ordered the immediate construction of a church on Tepeyac Hill. The woman appeared again, this time to Juan's gravely ill uncle. Not only was he healed in her presence, but she also revealed her name to him: the Holy Virgin Mother Mary of Guadalupe.

The image of Our Lady of Guadalupe is surrounded by mystery. It shows a brown mestiza Madonna in a coat adorned with stars, standing on a half-moon with the sun shining behind her. Her head is turned down and her eyes are half closed, as if to communicate solidarity with those who are downtrodden. The picture seems to be painted, but the material of the colors is unknown, and they appear to change depending on the angle at which they are viewed. The durability of the cape is also amazing, as cactus fibers do not last long. But this cape, now almost 500 years old, shows little signs of wear, especially considering it survived an accidental spill of acid in 1785 during a routine cleaning and a bomb, maliciously placed at its feet in the 1920s, that did significant damage to the surrounding building but left the tilma untouched.

Today when you come to the foot of Tepeyac Hill, which is now inside the city lines of Mexico City, you find several old buildings and beautiful landscaped gardens. The first basilica was constructed on the site of an earlier sixteenth-century church and was finished in 1709. When this basilica became dangerous due to the dramatic sinking of its foundations, a modern structure called the New Basilica was built next to it and the original image of the Virgin of Guadalupe was moved there.

The Basilica of Our Lady of Guadalupe is beautiful, unassuming, and somewhat overwhelming. One's eye is immediately swept upward toward the curves in the ceiling and drawn to the warm wood tones of the apse wall with its glistening golden adornment. As the eyes begin to focus, a thin golden cross takes form, and in the lower right corner of the cross, a golden glow surrounds a portrait. There, at the foot of the cross, is the miraculous image of the Virgin of Guadalupe.

Built in the 1970s, this new sacred space has the capacity to hold 10,000 worshipers. The nave is semi-circular with seven large, wide doors that swing open to the outside. Several aisles radiate out from the altar area like the rays of the sun, and Our Lady is visible from every angle. Further to the right of Our Lady and several feet in front of the apse wall is the icon of Juan Diego, kneeling before and listening to Mother Mary's message for him. Generous planters of flowers fill the altar space, and many visitors each day bring more flowers.

Large light installations swirl above the altar area on either side of the apse wall. From the entrance of the church, they seem dim. But

they change as one moves forward toward the altar. Light that shines through glass squares at the bottom of each individual light fixture has a glittering effect, and as the eyes gaze upward, they make a startling discovery: a skylight at the top of the apse wall. The overall effect is stunning, as the visitor moves from the shadows of the entrance into growing light.

The apse wall is immense, stretching from the skylight at the highest point of the building and descending into the lower crypt level. It is a beautiful representation of what Our Lady of Guadalupe means to those devoted to her—at once both of earth and of heaven, she meets anyone who will take the time to know her at the foot of the cross. She inhabits a special place in Indian and Hispanic culture. She is a peace icon, connecting different cultures, a coat of love to the desperate, and a sign of hope for the striving, making her basilica a place to address prayers and thanks. The old holy spaces on Tepeyac Hill may have been unknowingly built on shifting sand, but the foundation of faith of the Mexican people, with the help of Our Lady, stands firmly intact upon the Rock of Ages.

"I hereby command you: Be strong and courageous; do not be frightened or dismayed, for the LORD your God is with you wherever you go."

—Joshua 9:1

BASILICA OF OUR LADY
OF GUADALUPE

The old and new basilicas, Guadalupe

27

CATHEDRAL BASILICA OF SAINT LOUIS

A s vast as the universal Church can seem, the truth of any parish, great or small, lies within the context of its location. Situated in the center of a city whose geography is significant, the Cathedral Basilica of St. Louis contains stories told by the glorious golden mosaics seen on every one of its surfaces, which are rich with local history and the history of the Church at large.

The City of St. Louis is embedded in the heart of the Heartland of the United States. With fertile farmland in the surrounding area and nestled inside the bend of the mighty Mississippi River at the point where it converges with the Missouri River, St. Louis was a natural launching point for westward settlers and explorers alike, including the renowned expedition of Lewis and Clark. St. Louis's famous arch, which stands as the "Gateway to the West," commemorates this city's unique heritage in American history.

East meets West in St. Louis in more ways than in physical geography. At its founding in the mid-eighteenth century, French settler Pierre Laclede decided to name the city after a beloved medieval king, Louis IX, who was the only French monarch to achieve sainthood. He was known as a just, generous, and pious ruler, who died *en route* to his second crusade. From the city's earliest days, Roman Catholic priests and religious brothers and sisters were requested to come and establish infrastructure and education in the growing city. Schools, hospitals, and orphanages were built, and much of their legacy and influence brought from the old country can be found in this town located in the American

◀ *Nave, Cathedral Basilica of Saint Louis*

Midwest. It stands to reason, then, that such a community, bridging both geographical and cultural divides, would create a worship space that spans the ideas of Christianity.

Even as you approach the Cathedral Basilica in the heat and humidity of a St. Louis summer, all it takes is one step inside for it to become apparent that there is nothing typical about this overwhelmingly beautiful space. The first glance inside the enormous structure reveals a library of glittering mosaics in every direction and a central dome that commands visitors' attention; both of these are strikingly reminiscent of the amazing St. Mark's Basilica in Venice, Italy—a city with unique geography where ideas from the East and West also converged.

Archbishop Glennon, who spearheaded the building project after realizing that the old cathedral under the arch could no longer accommodate a large and growing Catholic population, proclaimed in the early twentieth century that this new cathedral of St. Louis would be the "Rome of the West." It contains one of the world's largest collections of Byzantine-style mosaics, with their bright colors and bold lines, that took more than seventy-five years to complete. The stories told in this painstaking art form range from the life of King Louis IX in the vestibule, to significant figures of the St. Louis community and ranks of angels displaying the words of the Beatitudes in the nave, to the biblical narrative and the life of Jesus in the transept and sanctuary. Capping the sweeping pictures that line the walls are a series of three domes familiar to the architecture of Eastern Orthodox Churches. A dome symbolizes heaven and often depicts Jesus as the Pantocrator, or ruler of the universe. Instead of one large image of Christ in the central dome, the cathedral contains several pictures in rich red and amber tones portraying the heavenly Jerusalem as told in the Book of Revelation. The dome that is the furthest north arches over the prominent high altar, decidedly of Western Roman influence, where the priest has always said Mass in full view of the congregation.

One of the most poignant mosaics found in the nave tells the story of Cardinal Ritter, who was the successor to Archbishop Glennon. Shortly after his arrival in St. Louis, he championed the cause begun

there by Glennon of desegregating the Catholic schools, something he had already established in his previous appointment in the Archdiocese of Indianapolis. When Cardinal Ritter learned there was a group of parishioners in the St. Louis area who were planning to sue the Archdiocese over the desegregation issue, he issued a pastoral letter that was read in every parish church at Sunday Mass stating clearly that anyone who pursued a lawsuit would be excommunicated. Needless to say, no one sued, and the Catholic schools of St. Louis were desegregated years before the Brown vs. Board of Education ruling made integration the law of the land. In similar fashion, Cardinal Ritter was again instrumental during the Second Vatican Council in the cause for recognizing the validity of the faith of denominations outside of Catholicism. The mosaic shows a group of Protestant ministers and a rabbi standing on one side of the cardinal and a teaching nun with a group of racially integrated children on the other.

With mission and education at its heart, this cathedral stands at a crossroads on many levels and is well poised to continue leading the Church for generations to come.

CATHEDRAL BASILICA
OF SAINT LOUIS

Holy Spirit mosaic, Cathedral Basilica of St. Louis

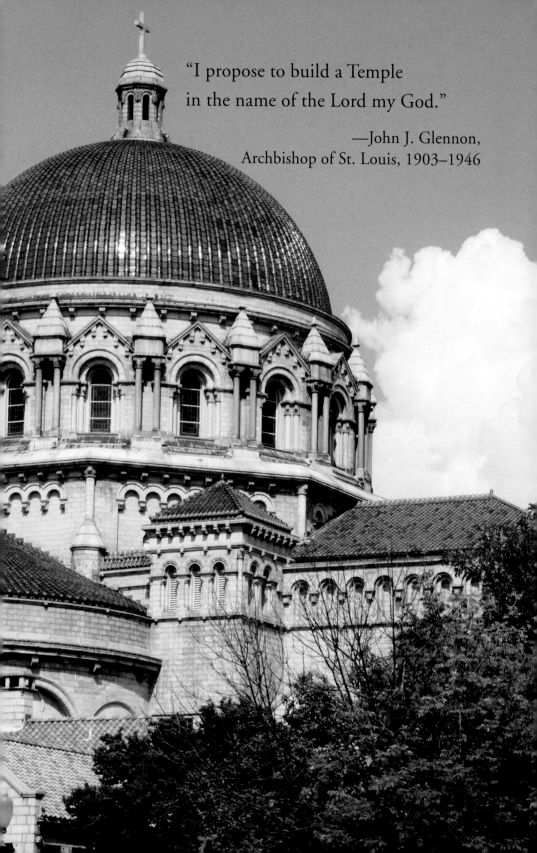

"I propose to build a Temple
in the name of the Lord my God."

—John J. Glennon,
Archbishop of St. Louis, 1903–1946

28

SOURCE OF INSPIRATION

The artists of the cathedrals have tried to work toward the highest possibilities of human craftsmanship, technique, and expressiveness. Many of the original architects, master builders, stonemasons, and glass artists remain unknown by name because they understood their work to be not an expression of personal artistry, but a gesture of a great common work for the glory of God, whose Spirit works through them.

The successful implementation of their creative gifts and profound understanding of harmony, aesthetics, and beauty have led to countless people's being drawn to these churches again and again, making cathedrals some of the most visited buildings in the world. A cathedral becomes a source of inspiration for future generations, as many visitors' hearts are imprinted and inspired by its figures, images, and stained glass. Pilgrims and spiritual seekers alike come back again and again because they feel that the aura of the cathedral is like a charging station for their soul.

When the architect Eugène Viollet-le-Duc was commissioned to carry out the renovation of the Notre-Dame Cathedral in Paris in the mid-nineteenth century, he wrote an interesting note in his construction diary. In his work with the South Rose Window, he noticed that the entire structure of the rose was by one degree out of balance, and noted that he had corrected this "mistake." Today, the question arises whether this deviation by one degree was actually a deliberate plan by the stonemasons of the Gothic

Dome, Cathedral Basilica of St. Louis

era. If one looks for a while at a picture that is a little bit out of balance, the brain itself compensates for this mistake. If one looks at it even longer and sinks into the picture, so to speak, it may happen that one has the impression that the circular rose would start to spin.

Some paintings or works of art are exactly this sort of invitation to "sink in." They are often designed so that not only is something visible in the initial glance, but also more is revealed in each hidden layer beyond the surface. Cathedrals on every continent are filled with elements that foster space for individuals to connect to hidden places within themselves, as well as to the larger story of life. Sometimes these elements are centrally placed and difficult not to notice within cathedral spaces, such as the Epiphany shrine in Cologne Cathedral, the image of Mary as Our Lady of Guadalupe in Mexico City, or the large rose windows of Chartres Cathedral. Sometimes they are unmistakably stretched above like the famous rib star suspended in the center tower of the transept of the Cathedral of Saint Mary of Burgos in Spain, or in the great domes of Ely or St. Peter's.

Sometimes, however, the special elements of a cathedral are hidden and discovered only by the person whose gaze or heart is magnetically drawn to a detail or element that reveals itself to that individual at that particular moment. It is a miracle to see something so beguiling that it triggers a great reverence for the human-made architectural masterpiece that surrounds us. But perhaps even more beguiling is the miracle of awakening to the idea that in every soul there is a divine spark, going beyond the scope and mastery of human art, that dwells and works within us.

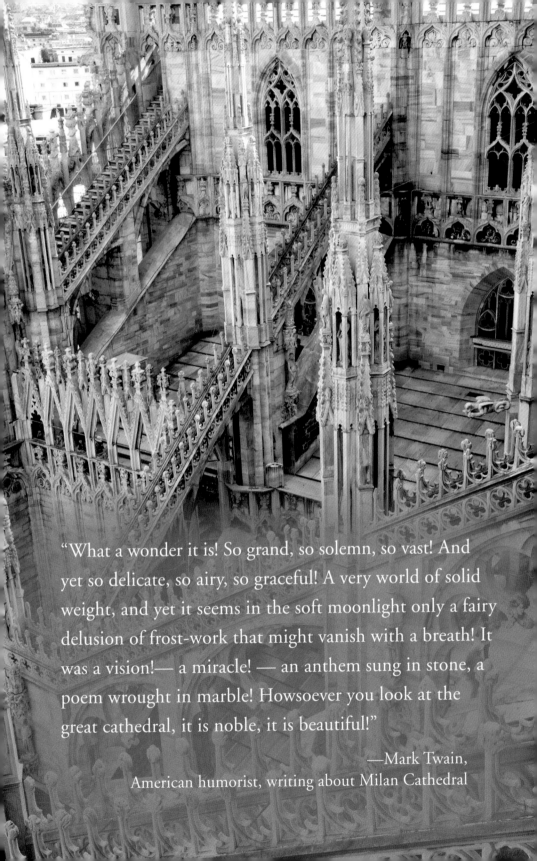

"What a wonder it is! So grand, so solemn, so vast! And yet so delicate, so airy, so graceful! A very world of solid weight, and yet it seems in the soft moonlight only a fairy delusion of frost-work that might vanish with a breath! It was a vision!— a miracle! — an anthem sung in stone, a poem wrought in marble! Howsoever you look at the great cathedral, it is noble, it is beautiful!"

—Mark Twain,
American humorist, writing about Milan Cathedral

29

HAGIA SOPHIA

In the two centuries after Christianity became sanctioned by the Roman Emperor Constantine, the liturgy of the church steadily became more elaborate and entwined with the nobility of the Byzantine Empire. In 532, the Emperor Justinian began construction on what would become the archetype for Byzantine church architecture and the ultimate expression of an active period of sacred art. In an astonishingly brief span of six years, the great church of Hagia Sophia (Greek for "Church of Holy Wisdom") was completed. On entering the newly opened cathedral in 537, Justinian is said to have exclaimed, "Glory to the Most High, who considered me worthy to complete such a work. Solomon, I have excelled you."

▲ *Hagia Sophia*

Hagia Sophia's brilliant construction, whose primary feature is a large and seemingly weightless dome, embodies the Orthodox theology of worship. Namely, this sacred space represents the whole cosmos and the interaction and nearness of God with God's creation. The dome is seen to be the heavens and the nave is the earth. There, worshipers would enter the kingdom of heaven and participate in creation's unending hymn of praise. For 900 years, Hagia Sophia served as the main cathedral of Constantinople. In 1453, when the Ottoman siege was imminent, members of the clergy gathered to hold one final Mass in the Great Church. By the following dawn, the troops of Sultan Mehmed II were laying waste to the city, and Hagia Sophia would never again be a church for Christians. Instead, the Ottomans converted the beautiful space, adding minarets and Islamic symbols, into their premiere mosque. It remained as such for nearly 500 years until 1931, when the Turkish government secularized the space and re-opened it in 1935 as a museum.

The name of a church, known as its patronage, is born of a vision of what its mission will be. This singular piece of real estate—in ancient times called Byzantium, later renamed Constantinople, in modern-day Istanbul—lies at the intersection of Orient and Occident, Europe and Asia, Latin West and Orthodox East, Christianity and Islam. It is no coincidence that in the heart of this cross-section of the old world Hagia Sophia is named for the second Person (Logos) of the Holy Trinity, and that its name means *Sacred Wisdom*. How interesting it is that throughout all the changes it endured in its long history, it is still known today by its original name and continues to stand as a beacon for hope in the world.

Hagia Sophia has existed for nearly 1500 years—another marvel, especially because it has survived several severe earthquakes. Structural cracks and partial collapses resulted, but the pillars and domes were able to be strengthened and rebuilt. Additionally, it endured the brunt of destructive attacks, most notably during the beginning of the Ottoman reign. Mosaics were destroyed or covered over; crosses and other Christian art and symbols were repurposed or plundered. Today, the partially crumbled plaster only gives an idea of how the church must have been in its full splendor. Visitors must use their imagination to picture the gilded domes that once inspired early pilgrims to give euphoric descriptions and write poetry.

Still, today the grandeur of the room and the large and inviting upper floors impress. Even more impressive, however, is the awe-inspiring realization that for centuries people from all over the world have come to pay their respects to this monument to sacred wisdom. In the marble of the balustrade, one sees traces of a visit from over a thousand years ago, where a Norman (Helvdan) literally left his mark. You can place your finger on the "pillar of tears" as a multitude of pilgrims have done before. Or, you may look into the eyes of one of the faces in the mosaics and wonder about the generations who have come to see this beauty. Standing beneath the dome, you sense the history and at the same time you understand that you have now become part of it. In this blessed centerpiece, for all the twists and turns of its fate, it remains the Hagia Sophia, the great patron saint of divine wisdom.

"Behold, she is a perpetual miracle. And on all the arches, as if carried by air, the vault spreads like the folds of a robe, and on its back the divine head of the middle is planted. As feathers rise into the air, the arches pierced through with multiple openings, enveloped in thin glass, through which brilliantly the rosy dawn flows in."

—Paulus Silentiarius,
poet in the service of Emperor Justinian I

HAGIA SOPHIA

30

PATRONS OF LIFE

Cathedrals are generous meeting rooms. They are designed to fit thousands of people at one time, for celebrating the great festivals of the church year. On a deeper level, though, in these spaces there is a heightened awareness of the Communion of Saints. It is a core tenant of Christian belief that all who have gone before, those present, and all who are yet to come are bound together as one in the Body of Christ.

Traditional notions of time are suspended in these magnificent places that have endured so much history and sheltered so many souls across the centuries, and the ability to stand alongside our heroes in faith becomes a little more possible. The veil that separates the here and the hereafter thins, so to speak; these are "liminal" spaces. Of course, those whose images and stories are depicted in stone and glass are present in a special way: priests and prophets, apostles and saints, mothers and fathers, kings and queens. The truth of their lives and all the issues they faced are on display to stand as a gentle encouragement to us who are currently dealing with life's problems. These ancestors in the faith inspire and strengthen us to keep going around life's next curve.

For each cathedral, a special patron saint is chosen after whom it is named. This often intuitively addresses a main topic. The Cologne Cathedral of St. Peter, for example, is committed to the strength and authority of the Apostle Peter and, through the relics of the Magi, also to the wisdom of the East.

The young martyr Modesta, Chartres ▶

St. Stephen's Cathedral in Vienna stands for the inner fire and the devotion of the first martyr of the faith and calls all of us to preserve inner strength and conviction for the faith. Coventry, whose cathedral was destroyed by the human destructive power of war, is dedicated to the Archangel Michael, who guards the entrance to paradise with a fiery sword. It reminds us of the lost paradise of humans, but it also sends a signal to the world to demand peace with the determination of St. Michael. Ely Cathedral is a hymn to the great mystery of the Trinity, while Sagrada Familia calls the power and importance of the family into the twenty-first century.

Vézelay is dedicated to St. Mary Magdalene, recalling the importance of closeness and tenderness. Notre-Dame of Paris, and all churches dedicated to Mary, ask all who enter to remember the Mother to whom the faithful pray daily for assistance. These cathedrals join in the great Ave Maria, singing about the manifold and central importance of Motherhood.

Ulm Minster symbolizes the inner themes of the building itself, whose large tower is erected as high as a sky pillar, a lighthouse in the name of freedom and faith.

Not just the patron saints of the churches, but every single picture and figure tells a story with which we can orient ourselves. Each of their stories is in some way about trust and compassion, love and humility, greatness and justice. They are all invitations to increase trust in our own path in life and take the inspiration and blessing of the patrons we need for a successful journey.

"Being his workmanship doesn't mean we are all poets. It means we are all poems, individual created works of a creative God. "

—Emily P. Freeman,
American author and podcast host

31

ST. PETER'S BASILICA

The first St. Peter's Basilica was built around 324 on behalf of Emperor Constantine over the tomb of Peter, who was martyred in Rome. More than 1,000 years later, when a major refurbishment became inevitable, the decision was made to completely start new, and the old church was demolished.

The first master builder was Donato Bramante, but it was not until four popes later and the commissioning of Michelangelo, who had just painted the Sistine Chapel, as architect that momentum came into full swing. In 1547, Michelangelo completed his designs. In addition to the grandiose overall concept, his large dome is a special architectural masterpiece. Some two hundred years later, the entire construction was finally complete.

St. Peter's Basilica is in several ways the largest church in the world. The decoration, the mosaics and pictures, the dome, and the bronze canopy that arches over the tomb of the Apostle Peter make a stunning impression in the huge space. But despite all the grandeur and splendor, the basilica does not seem overloaded, but remains balanced and elegant in its proportions.

From the central window, the dove of the Holy Spirit shines into the nave, like a reminder that all human greatness relates to the divine gift of the Spirit. The four pillars supporting the dome are dedicated to four somewhat unlikely people: Helena, Veronica, Longinus, and Andrew, who, though not at the center of salvation history, through their expression of faith are

◀ *Michelangelo's dome, St. Peter's Basilica*

symbolic of humanity. Helena, the mother of Emperor Constantine, stands for the possibility of salvation for the powerful and wise. Veronica recalls the compassionate caring that wiped away the sweat of the suffering Christ with her cloth. Longinus was a Roman soldier who jabbed the lance into Jesus's side in dutiful obedience, but then he realized the actual dimension of what he witnessed, and a profession of faith poured out of his soul and mouth.

> Now when the centurion and those with him, who were keeping watch over Jesus, saw the earthquake and what took place, they were terrified and said, "Truly this man was God's Son!" (Matthew 27:54)

Andrew, an apostle of Jesus, was exemplary in giving the fullest measure that humans can give, his life. All the popes who are present in St. Peter's Basilica—sometimes modest, sometimes grandiose— must measure their actions and keep in mind these four pillars of human dimension, which are not only for them, but for all who visit.

As the spiritual center of worldwide Catholicism, St. Peter's is the most recognized and best-known church of all. It focuses on the history of humanity and faith, which is perhaps succinctly experienced in the sense of awe pilgrims surely feel in the midst of this historic place.

Interior, St. Peter's Basilica

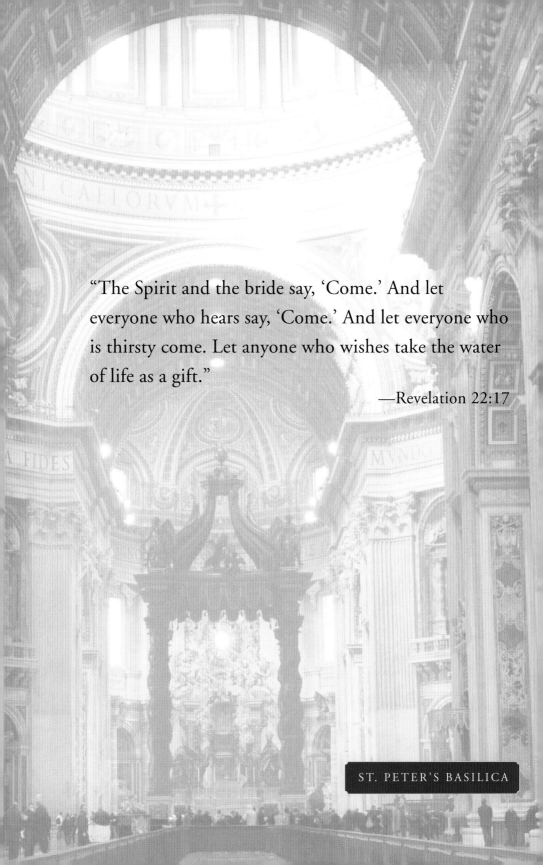

"The Spirit and the bride say, 'Come.' And let everyone who hears say, 'Come.' And let everyone who is thirsty come. Let anyone who wishes take the water of life as a gift."

—Revelation 22:17

ST. PETER'S BASILICA

32

CELEBRATION

When we sit down at a table, the preparation and environment are at least as important as the food itself. Tablecloth, crockery, cutlery and glasses, candles, the mood, friendliness, and attentiveness of the service play an essential role. These things, as well as how the food is presented on the plate, contribute to the enjoyment of the meal. Similarly, one can worship anywhere, but elements such as space, light, songs, smells, liturgy, garments, and choreography remain essential. Celebrating a festive service in a cathedral has something uplifting about it.

Before a celebration begins in a cathedral, the sound of the ringing bell suggests something significant. For some time, it was customary in many cathedrals on certain feast days that the congregation would enter through the side entrances instead of the main doors at the back of the nave. Once everyone was gathered inside, after the bell stopped ringing the bishop would knock his staff against the large center doors. Only then were the huge doors pushed open, allowing the light to flood inside. The entrance song would begin with organ and singing, and the procession of the celebrant and the servers would make its way down the aisle, the energy and excitement palpable.

Celebrating a service in all its liturgical details may sometimes seem exaggerated, but hardly anyone can escape the magic of such deliberate and often grand festivity. The encounter between God and God's people, the listening to the Word, the reverberation of emotions in song and worship, the celebration of belonging to the salvific event, the blessing promised—these have always inspired people to create a framework of the highest artistic design, to stretch the gifts of artisans to their furthermost point, and bring it into being.

Church buildings, like the sacred spaces of every culture, have always been attempts to express the divine spirit in and around us. People have felt their inner creative power and tried to create the most beautiful thing that can come from this spirit.

The description of the New Jerusalem in the Revelation to St. John (chapter 21) has particularly inspired cathedral builders through the ages. To bring the idea of the New Jerusalem on earth was their ideal. Lighting effects for the domes and floors were an attempt to bring about the glow of heaven. The golden floor could be created by polished stones or light effects, as the sparkling and translucent gems are reflected in the various colors of light streaming through the glass windows.

To be bigger, more beautiful, and nobler, too, was their challenge. Particularly in Gothic architecture, builders and architects ventured into new construction limits in ceiling height and increasingly large windows. And, after failing on numerous occasions, they tried again. Technical possibilities and decorating tastes inevitably changed, with fresh ideas springing up with new generations. In Constantinople or Rome, it was the size of the dome that was most impressive; in Barcelona, the plantlike pursuit of heaven was a fitting expression. Regardless of the detail, the goal was to do something greater and grander than had been done before, for the purpose of inspiring and uplifting the faithful and, indeed, all who entered. They wanted to create a space that aroused awe, wonder, and joy and gratitude for the gift of life, faith, and each one's place within the history of salvation.

Sainte-Chapelle, Paris ▶

Be aware, from now on, you yourself are the
intersection of heaven and earth, you who, inebriated
by the colors of paradise and touched by the sounds
of the Celestial City, have a new look at all things
that surround you."

—Jan Peter Marthe,
Austrian musician and conductor

CELEBRATION

AFTERWORD
We Have a Home

Home has many levels. We are at home in our bodies, in a house, neighborhood, village, country, or on our planet. Our homeland is where we feel accepted and welcomed. Home is where we belong. At the same time, our soul is enigmatically structured and gives us the first and innermost layer of home. There are people that we connect and feel comfortable with over the course of our lives, and they become our second layer of feeling at home.

Then there are the places we inhabit, either found in nature or designed by humans. Our comfort level in these places is sometimes affected by the outer circumstances of how well the space is cared for or the kind of energy that was left behind by others. Becoming attuned to this subtle awareness can lead to a heartfelt sympathy or even to the feeling of having always known and loved one another. This translates to our experiences in cathedrals.

When people say that Chartres Cathedral is as cozy as a living room, or the entrance into St. Stephen's Cathedral or Cologne Cathedral causes them to feel as if the church gives them a warm hug, or when people arrive in Santiago de Compostela or at Tepeyac Hill and feel relieved by age-old travel—this means these places convey the feeling of home to the human soul.

Perhaps it is the involvement in the great history of these places, or the pleasure in their artistry that makes us feel this way. Perhaps it is the harmonious structure or the implemented rules of aesthetics that produce an echo, a resonance within oneself. The solemnity, beauty, and even the generosity of talent and treasure of previous generations remind us of the grandeur of creation, the peculiarity of existence, and the great space of our souls.

◁ *The approach to Reims Cathedral*

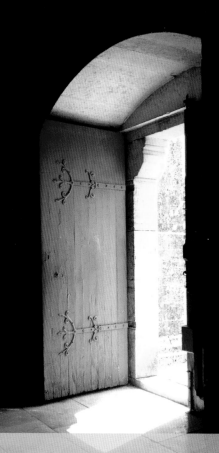

These must be some of the reasons why we feel not only cozy and safe at a kitchen table, but also inside a cathedral.

Do any of these cathedrals "call your name" or compel you to make your own visit or pilgrimage? What other places do you know that invite further exploration? Whether they are in your home country or across the globe, they await your discovery. May you be blessed as you go forward, changed by what you find, and pass on to others that which inspires you.

ACKNOWLEDGMENTS

Sources of quotations at the end of the chapters:

Introduction: Orson Welles, from the film *F for Fake*, 1973.

1 Theodor Fontane, *Briefe*, Wikiquote.

2 Robert A. Scott, *The Gothic Enterprise: A Guide to Understanding the Medieval Cathedral* (Berkeley, CA: University of California Press, 2003), 125.

3 Christoph Schönborn, *Die Kathedrale* (Freiburg: Herder, 2017), 20. Our translation.

4 Randolph M. Hollerith, *The Self-guided Tour at Washington National Cathedral* (Washington, DC: Washington National Cathedral, 2018), 1.

5 Reims, parisontheway.com/guided-tours-france/french-monuments-visits/notre-dame-de-reims-cathedral.html.

9 Helge Burggrabe, *Songbook Hagios I&II* (Fischerhude: Burggrabe, 2018), 34. Our translation.

10 Grace Hazard Conkling, from *A Treasury of War Poetry*, 1917.

11 Auguste Rodin, *Les Cathédrales de France* (Armand Colin, 1914), 123. Our translation.

12 Abbot Suger from Saint-Denis, translation of The Medieval Internet Sourcebook, https://sourcebooks.fordham.edu/source/sugar.asp.

13 Edward Matchett poem, in Painton Cowen, *Rose Windows* (San Francisco: Chronicle Books, 1979), 6.

14 Robert Barron, *Heaven in Stone and Glass: Experiencing the Spirituality of the Gothic Cathedrals* (New York: The Crossroad Publishing Company, 2000), 53.

15 John O'Donohue, *Beauty: The Invisible Embrace,* (New York: Harper Perennial, 2005), 82.

16 William Anderson, *The Rise of the Gothic* (Salem, MA: Salem House, 1988), 162.

17 Roger Willemsen, from roger-willemsen.de. Our translation.

18 James O'Donell, *Notre-Dame de Montréal* (Montréal: Basilique Notre-Dame, 2008), 61.

19 Antoine de St. Exupéry, *Le Petit Prince* (original edition Gallimard, 1946; bilingual edition Omilia Languages, 2001), 79.

20 Victor Hugo, public domain.

21 Paula D'Arcy, *Stars at Night: When Darkness Unfolds as Light* (Cincinnati: Franciscan Media, 2016), 91.

22 Robert Louis Stevenson, public domain.

23 St. Patrick, public domain.

24 Paulo Coelho, *The Alchemist* (New York: Harper Collins, 1983), 29.

25 Julie Roux, *The Roads to Santiago de Compostela* (Vic-en-Bigorre: MSM, 2007), 52.

27 Archbishop John Glennon, Cathedral Basilica of St. Louis Mosaic Museum, from a sermon preached in 1905.

28 Mark Twain, from *The Innocents Abroad.*

30 Emily P. Freeman, *A Million Little Ways* (Grand Rapids, MI: Revell, 2013), 29.

32 Jan Peter Marthe, *Die Heilige Messe* (Würzburg: Echter, 2011), 211. Our translation.

The authors want to thank the wonderful people at Paraclete Press who were so dedicated and spirit-filled in their work, especially Mark Burrows, who first offered the possibility of making this book; our editor Jon M. Sweeney; managing editor Robert Edmonson; marketing director Laura McKendree; and the graphic designers.

We also appreciate the help of the people who told us about their cathedrals and churches and offered insight and feedback about their chapters: Kevin Eckstrom, Chief Communications Officer of Washington National Cathedral; Lucie Kechichian, Communication Adviser of Notre Dame de Montreal; Mercedes Anderson, Office of Communications, St. Patrick, New York; Pat Donnelly, csj, Tourism and Gift Shop, Cathedral Basilica of St. Louis; Lauren Artress, Canon of Grace Cathedral.

We thank all those who supported us with pictures and stories from their archives and knowledge, especially Gilles Fresson, Historien et intendant de la cathédrale de Chartres; Andy Bittner, Docent of Washington National Cathedral; and again, Lauren Artress, Canon of Grace Cathedral.

We thank Helge Burggrabe, German musician and composer of great oratorios and songs who contributed the text of chapter 21, "The Cathedral as Music," to this book. (burggrabe.de)

ABOUT THE AUTHORS

Gernot Candolini, born 1959, lives in Innsbruck, Austria, and is headmaster of the Montessori School of Innsbruck. He is a leading labyrinth builder in Europe and author of several books. He returns every year to Chartres Cathedral where he leads groups in retreats to experience this place. (labyrinthe.at)

Jennifer Brandon, born 1977, is a music teacher and singer in Indianapolis, Indiana. Her own pilgrimage to Chartres was life-changing, and ever since, she loves to walk alongside other pilgrims to encourage their own transformation experiences. (apilgrimintheworld.com)

PHOTO CREDITS

Cᴏᴠᴇʀ: Andrew Bittner, Washington; Back cover: Justin Black, Shutterstock.com; endleaf papers: Reinhold Armbruster-Mayer, Ulm/D; p 4 Triff, Shutterstock.com; p 6/7 Henri de Feraudy, Rectorat Cathédrale de Chartres; p 8, 38/39, 67, 70/71, 73 Gilles Fresson, Rectorat Cathédrale de Chartres; p 9, 19, 30, 32, 33, 34, 35, 40, 46, 55, 59, 60/61, 62, 64, 68/69, 72, 90, 92, 93, 94, 104, 107, 113, 114, 116, 118/119, 122/123, 128, 131, 146/147, 156, 158/59, 162, 164, 165 Gernot Candolini; p 10 matthi, Shutterstock.com; p 13 Elya, Wikimedia commons; p 14 Jorg Hackemann, Shutterstock.com; p 16 Charles Hummel, synergia-verlag.ch; p 20 TTstudio, Shutterstock.com; p 22/23 ppl, Shutterstock.com; p 24 Washington National Cathedral; p 29 Andrew Bittner, Washington; p 36 Paula Candolini; p 42/43 Chantal Himmele; p 45 carmelite.org; p 51 Light dots on the floor Francis Verillon, Wikimedia Commons; p 26, 50, 52/53, 54, 74, 87, 88, 95, 106, 141, 142, 148, 151, 152, 161, 166, 169, 172 Jennifer Brandon; p 56 David Foster, Creativecommons.org; p 58 katholisch.atp; p 76, 80/81 © The Community of Jesus, Inc.; p 78/79 © 2011 Robert Benson Photography; p 82 TTstudio, Shutterstock .com; p 85 Vlad G, Shutterstock.com; p 96, 99 David Iliff, Wikimedia Commons; p 102 Lars Howlett - discoverlabyrinths.com; p 108, 111 Basilica Notre-Dame, Montréal, Alain Régimbald; p 124/125, 127 Reinhold Armbruster-Mayer, Ulm/D; p 132 Ivanko Filimonov, Shutterstock.com; p 135 quehacerensantiago .com; p 136/137, 138/139 istockphotos.com; p 155 Rob van Esch, Shutterstock.com; p 168/169 Justin Black, Shutterstock.com; p 170 yurikov, shutterstock.com

ABOUT PARACLETE PRESS

Who We Are

As the publishing arm of the Community of Jesus, Paraclete Press presents a full expression of Christian belief and practice—from Catholic to Evangelical, from Protestant to Orthodox, reflecting the ecumenical charism of the Community and its dedication to sacred music, the fine arts, and the written word. We publish books, recordings, sheet music, and video/DVDs that nourish the vibrant life of the church and its people.

What We Are Doing

Books

PARACLETE PRESS BOOKS show the richness and depth of what it means to be Christian. While Benedictine spirituality is at the heart of who we are and all that we do, our books reflect the Christian experience across many cultures, time periods, and houses of worship.

We have many series, including *Paraclete Essentials*; *Paraclete Fiction*; *Paraclete Poetry*; *Paraclete Giants*; and for children and adults, *All God's Creatures*, books about animals and faith; and *San Damiano Books*, focusing on Franciscan spirituality. Others include *Voices from the Monastery* (men and women monastics writing about living a spiritual life today), *Active Prayer*, and new for young readers: *The Pope's Cat*. We also specialize in gift books for children on the occasions of Baptism and First Communion, as well as other important times in a child's life, and books that bring creativity and liveliness to any adult spiritual life.

The MOUNT TABOR BOOKS series focuses on the arts and literature as well as liturgical worship and spirituality; it was created in conjunction with the Mount Tabor Ecumenical Centre for Art and Spirituality in Barga, Italy.

Music

The PARACLETE RECORDINGS label represents the internationally acclaimed choir *Gloriæ Dei Cantores*, the *Gloriæ Dei Cantores Schola*, and the other instrumental artists of the *Arts Empowering Life Foundation*.

Paraclete Press is the exclusive North American distributor for the Gregorian chant recordings from St. Peter's Abbey in Solesmes, France. Paraclete also carries all of the Solesmes chant publications for Mass and the Divine Office, as well as their academic research publications.

In addition, PARACLETE PRESS SHEET MUSIC publishes the work of today's finest composers of sacred choral music, annually reviewing over 1,000 works and releasing between 40 and 60 works for both choir and organ.

Video

Our video/DVDs offer spiritual help, healing, and biblical guidance for a broad range of life issues including grief and loss, marriage, forgiveness, facing death, understanding suicide, bullying, addictions, Alzheimer's, and Christian formation.

Learn more about us at our website:
www.paracletepress.com

or phone us toll-free at 1.800.451.5006

SCAN
TO READ
MORE

ALSO AVAILABLE
from Mount Tabor Books at Paraclete Press

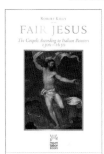

FAIR JESUS
The Gospels According to Italian Painters 1300–1650
Robert Kiely
ISBN 978-1-64060-258-8 | $39.99, Hardcover

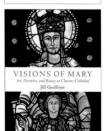

VISIONS OF MARY
Art, Devotion, and Beauty at Chartres Cathedral
Jill K. H. Geoffrion
ISBN 978-1-61261-894-4 | $29.99, Hardcover

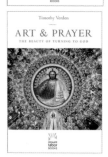

ART & PRAYER
The Beauty of Turning to God
Timothy Verdon
ISBN 978-1-64060-423-0 | $29.99, Trade paperback

THE ECUMENISM OF BEAUTY
Edited by Timothy Verdon
ISBN 978-1-61261-924-8 | $28.99, Hardcover

Available at bookstores
Paraclete Press | 1-800-451-5006
For the complete Mount Tabor Collection visit www.paracletepress.com